GIRARDI

Passion in Pinstripes

KEVIN KERNAN

TRIUMPH
BOOKS

Library of Congress Cataloging-in-Publication Data

Kernan, Kevin, 1953–
    Girardi: passion in pinstripes / Kevin Kernan.
        p. cm.
    ISBN 978-1-60078-582-5 (hardback)
    1. Girardi, Joe. 2. Baseball managers—United States—Biography.
3. Conduct of life. 4. New York Yankees (Baseball team) I. Title.
    GV865.G57K47 2012
    796.357092—dc23
    [B]
                                                      2012000158

This book is available in quantity at special discounts for your group or organization. For further information, contact:

    Triumph Books LLC
    542 South Dearborn Street, Suite 750
    Chicago, Illinois 60605
    (312) 939-3330
    Fax (312) 663-3557
    www.triumphbooks.com

Printed in U.S.A.
ISBN: 978-1-60078-582-5
Design and editorial production by Prologue Publishing Services, LLC
Photos courtesy of AP Images unless otherwise indicated

Thank God for the greatest editor of all, my wife, Anne. Throughout my conversations with Joe Girardi, he was never hesitant to praise his wife, Kim, for her tremendous devotion as a wife, mother, friend, and counselor. I know just how he feels.

CONTENTS

1.

TIME IN A BOTTLE

WHEN JOE GIRARDI talks about his dad, it is with reverence and pride. The lessons he learned from his father, Jerry, will be with him for the rest of his life, and he continues to pass those lessons on to his own children.

The greatest lessons can come along in the most ordinary of circumstances. That is what truly makes them so special, so powerful, and so memorable. If you really want to know about Jerry Girardi, all you have to do is listen to Joe tell the following story about his dad. It is a small story, but it says so much. It tells you where the son gets his inner strength and how Joe was able to play 15 years in the majors at the most difficult position, catcher. It tells you about Joe's determination as a player and as a manager.

If you don't make the postseason your first year as Yankees manager in 2008, you find a way to make it to the playoffs the following year and win the Yankees' 27th world championship. You may not make it to the World Series, but you always finish what you start, no matter how difficult the circumstances, no matter what obstacles may come your way.

"I saw my father do something I will never forget when he was adding the addition to our house," Joe began. "He was working on the faucet in the bathtub, and he had one of those big plumber's wrenches, and he smashed his thumb. His thumb was bleeding all over the place—he actually broke it—and he just put tape around his thumb and finished the job first. That's who my dad was."

That's Jerry Girardi. That's also Joe and all his siblings—John, George, Jerry, and Maria. Finish the job. Do the best you can do with the equipment you have. If you smash your thumb, you tape it up and move on. Don't make excuses. If something goes wrong, work to the best of your ability to correct the situation. Finish what you started.

Everyday life really is about smashing your thumb.

Perseverance may be the greatest lesson any father can teach a son or daughter. No matter what obstacles get in the way, finish the job. Jerry Girardi has long suffered from Alzheimer's, and Girardi longs for the days when he could sit and have a conversation with his dad. He wishes his children would know their grandfather as he knew the man. He wishes he could do the simplest things with his dad, who has struggled through this dark time for many years.

"I really miss fishing with my dad," Girardi said of the wonderful simple acts their relationship was built upon. "That's one thing as a father and a son that you can always do. The days of playing basketball or playing baseball, those days are over, but you could always fish together."

Just throw a couple of lines in the water and talk and enjoy the time together. Despite the cruelty of Alzheimer's, Joe makes the best of those times when he is able to visit his dad, who is in a full-care facility, not far from where Joe grew up in East Peoria, Illinois. Whenever the Yankees are in Chicago during the season, Joe makes the trip to see his dad. After the season is complete, he makes sure to visit as often as he can, and through it all, he knows his father is getting the best care available.

"They do a really great job with my dad," Joe said with emotion in his voice. "My concern would be that he is skinny and frail, but every time I go he's been fed and he seems strong."

As he makes the two-and-a-half-hour drive to see his dad, Joe thinks of the good times as a family. He thinks of his mom and dad and growing up and all the people who were there to help him in his life. He thinks of how his mother battled ovarian cancer for six years. When Joe was 13, Angela Girardi was diagnosed with cancer and given three to six months to live. She lived another six years. Her spirit lives on in Joe every day in the final words she told him: "Don't forget me." He never will.

He thinks of those long summer days when he played with his good friend, Todd Mervosh, the games they played and all the peanut butter and jelly sandwiches Todd's mom, Phyllis, used to make for them every day at Todd's house. The two friends lived five houses from each other on Oakwood Road, and Todd's house offered the perfect side yard in which to play all day long.

Todd, now a scientist working for the state of Connecticut, remembers those days fondly as well. "We played everything from Wiffle ball to badminton to croquet to touch football there," Todd said. "For a period of time, Joe was my closest friend."

Joe was a Cubs fan. Todd was a Cardinals fan. "We'd trade baseball cards," Todd said. "He'd have a Lou Brock; I'd have a Billy Williams. We'd trade so I could get the Cardinals players and he could get the Cubs." Todd also remembers the toughness of Joe. The yard was ringed by a honeysuckle hedge. One day Todd's dad trimmed the hedge, leaving some sharp edges. Joe went back to make a catch during a Wiffle ball game and ran smack into the hedges. "Joe had his mouth open, and he crashed into the hedge and cut the inside of his mouth really badly with the cut end of the hedge," Todd recalled. "Joe made the catch, his mouth was bleeding all over the place; my mom came rushing out to take care of him. He didn't even cry. He was just a tough kid. If that had been me, I probably would have been bawling my head off."

On a recent trip back home, Joe stopped to see Mrs. Mervosh, and, yes, she offered him a peanut butter and jelly sandwich just like when he was a youngster.

"She was working on her Christmas tree, so I didn't want to bother her," Joe said with a smile. "I think about the way she took care of me as a little boy, I'd play with Todd all day. It was like being in a camp." He then added, "I really missed the times we grew up. I used to ride my bike to baseball practice, which was five miles away, and Mr. Mervosh would bring me home in his mail truck. Our practices were from about 3:00 to 5:00, and when he got off work, he would take us right home."

Just put the bike into the truck and climb aboard. Todd, who played with Joe later on the Sea Merchants travel baseball team, said years later that his dad, Ted, who passed away in 2008, would say that he did not cart Joe home in the mail truck, noting that his dad would comment, "Oh, no, I was always careful never to use the mail truck."

Personal truck or mail truck, everyone looked out for each other in that community, and in many ways people are still looking out for Joe and his family.

"Sometimes it's just me when I visit my dad and sometimes the family goes," Girardi said of his trips to see Jerry. "My father doesn't really speak anymore, but it seems that the times that I bring my kids, he'll say something. Now it doesn't necessarily make sense, but he'll say something. Whatever it is in the kids' voices, it will always trigger something in him. It's great.

"His friends visit him, which is great. Judy, to me, is our little angel."

Judy Shea is there to help Jerry Girardi nearly every day. "Many years after my mom passed away, my dad started dating Judy," Joe explained. "They were basically together for 10 years before he went into the home. She took care of my dad. She traveled with him. She took him to Italy, where he got to see where he grew up. She's amazing. And she goes and sees him probably five days a week."

With Joe and his wife, Kim, being so far away, that is a blessing.

"As I see my dad, and as I get older, I realize that I'm really a lot like my dad," Joe said. "I realize how much I look like my father now that I never really saw in the past. I realize that the time that I spent with my kids is really what I saw my father do."

Joe is his father's son. Jerry Girardi was the perfect role model for Joe, and that is why Joe loves to spend time with his children. During a weekend visit to New York City in November to take care of some business, Joe said he had to hurry back to his home in Westchester to help coach his son Dante's football team. It is always about family. "My father took me to work, and that's why I'm a big believer in allowing players to take their kids to work—because I saw what my dad did and I enjoyed it," Joe said.

Even if it is not his own kids at the game, Girardi goes out of his way to take care of them. Aris Sakellaridis, a retired New York City corrections officer and good friends with Hank Steinbrenner, is a freelance writer and photographer who authored the book *Yankees Retired Numbers*. One day a charity that Sakellaridis was associated with brought a young man to Yankee Stadium to be an honorary batboy for the game. About a half hour before the game, Girardi sat the youngster, who was about 10 years old, in his office as he scanned the Yankees lineup. Joe handed the lineup card to the youngster and said, "How's that look to you?"

"That was priceless," Sakellaridis explained. "The kid felt a part of it, like he had something to do with that lineup that day. Girardi treated the kid as if he were his own son. You watch Girardi every day when he steps out on that field for batting practice. He will always go behind that rope to sign autographs or pose with the kids for pictures. He'll never just come out and go straight to the cage. He'll always spend time with those kids. Joe is as real as they come."

That is how he treats his players, as well, he is there for them. This is the essence of his philosophy. He wants his players as healthy as possible for the postseason. That is the goal. "I'm not going to hurt someone to win a series," Girardi explained. "The important thing is that we stay healthy.... The goal here is to not just make the playoffs. The goal here is to win the World Series, and you have to have healthy players to do that."

For the last four years, the Yankees have run an award-winning program called Hope Week, and Girardi takes an active role each year in offering hope to those in need. For five consecutive days during Hope Week, the Yankees shine the spotlight on a different individual, family, or organization worthy of recognition and support. The outreach usually takes place at a community location and ends with a visit to Yankee Stadium.

The event can be anything from a double-decker bus ride around New York with refugees from Haiti who endured the devastating earthquake (a trip that included the participants lighting the tower of the Empire State Building), to a day at the beach with Tuesday's Children (children who lost a parent on 9/11), or it can be a trip to the ballpark with a lifelong Yankees fan who has been blind since birth.

"If we were going to do this," explained Jason Zillo, Yankees director of communications and media relations, "we wanted everyone to be invested in this." That included the Big Four of Girardi, GM Brian Cashman, Yankees president Randy Levine, and chief operating officer Lonn Trost. "I went to Joe first and presented it to him—without his blessing I was not going any further," Zillo said. "He embraced the concept. He loved the fact that it was something different and that the players were going to be able to work together on some of these days with random pairings of players. He thought that would be a great way for our guys to kind of get away from the ballpark and spend two or three hours together on something that is pretty meaningful. He just said, 'What do you need from me? Because I want to see this thing happen.'

"This is a lot to take in because you are talking about five straight days, and you don't want to do anything to interfere with these guys' preparation," Zillo added. It also shows that the Evil Empire is not so evil. One of the events in 2010 had Girardi, Joba Chamberlain, David Robertson, Chad Gaudin, and Tino Martinez make the trip from New Jersey to Yankee Stadium with a blind fan named Jane Lang, 67, and her guide dog, Clipper. The group took each step of the way of the more-than-two-hour journey that Jane usually takes when she goes to the ballpark, including the walk from her home in Morris Plains, New Jersey, to her local train station for the ride to New York, getting into Manhattan, and then taking the subway to the Bronx and Yankee Stadium. At the end of the day, Girardi made Jane's day by guiding her around the bases for her home run.

"That was one of the most powerful things when he walked Jane Lang around the bases," Zillo said. "When she touched home plate with Joe holding her, it was awesome."

Girardi insisted that each day the Hope Week participants bring the lineup card to home plate before the game. "Joe brings up hope every year because he believes hope is what allowed him to spend as much time as he did with his mother," Zillo said. "She wanted to see her kids graduate."

Hope is a powerful thing. Girardi's charity is the Catch 25 Foundation, and he said, "It's a foundation based on giving people hope." Even though he has had so many accomplishments throughout his life already, Girardi jokes that he is the black sheep of his family because of his highly educated siblings. "My two old-est brothers are doctors, and my sister is a professor," he said. "My other brother is an accountant. For me, four years of college was enough, and I'm really happy with what I do."

He was happy with his playing career, his broadcasting career, and now his managerial career. He loves being a father and a husband, recently celebrating his 22nd wedding anniversary with Kim, the girl he met in college, the girl he knew he would marry back when her name was Kim Innocenzi. "We laugh at how fast the time has gone because we've known each other longer than we haven't known each other," Girardi said.

Being a father means the world to Girardi, and it all comes back to being with his own dad and the great times they had in work and in play, the lessons learned, the time spent together.

"I had a great example in my father where it was about us," Girardi said. "It was making sure we did well in school, making sure we had fun playing athletics. Making sure that he had time for us whether he was taking us with on his job or whatever it was.

"Kim's always got the kids and makes sure we are together and everything is always right. I want them to know what we do. I want them to be a part of this. I ask them, 'Are you okay with Daddy doing this?'"

And if they weren't, if it were best for his family to leave the game of baseball, Girardi vowed, "I would walk away." That is not happening. Everyone in the Girardi family loves the game. That is something that developed, the love of baseball that Joe's father taught him.

"My dad was the one who really taught me the game," Girardi said. "We'd sit down at home, and he'd teach me the game. My father was a salesman, and there were days I would ride in the car with him. I don't know if I acted good or bad when we were at the sales calls, but we would listen to the Cubs games on the radio because they were day games. We'd listen to Jack Brickhouse and Lou Boudreau. And then when they were on the road, we'd sit in the family room and watch them on TV."

Jerry Girardi was into every pitch. "My father could get a little upset if they didn't play well," Joe said. Jerry, of course, had plenty of chances to get upset. Those Cubs did not play well a lot of the time. "He brainwashed me to be a Cubs fan from when I was a little boy, and I know he's still waiting for them to win," Joe said with a smile.

Maybe someday the Cubs will win a World Series again, something that hasn't happened since 1908. Even for Cubs fans, there is always hope.

There are so many lessons Girardi learned from his dad. Shortly before the Yankees played the Cubs in a weekend series in Chicago in June 2011, Girardi told Jack Curry on *The Joe Girardi Show* the impact his father had on him: "When I think of my father, I think of two things: the value of hard work and toughness. My father wanted us to know what he did, and my father worked three jobs to support the five children. He would take me on the weekend to be the laborer. He would lay bricks on the weekend. He would pay me for my work and taught me the value of money. We would work hard. For a seven-year-old to be carrying bricks and to be mixing the mortar and to be smoothing out in between the layers, it was a great experience for me."

That work experience made Joe strong, it made him pay attention to detail, and to do the job the right way. "The other thing he taught me about was toughness," Girardi said. There were plenty of opportunities for that. Sports were the perfect outlet for Jerry Girardi to teach his son about toughness. They would wrestle. Wrestling was big in the Girardi family. "My dad's brother was a longtime wrestling coach at Illinois State," Girardi said. "But I never wrestled. Only my older brother did, one year."

They would play basketball—tough, physical basketball. "We would play basketball in the backyard, and he would push me around," Girardi said. "When I would shoot, he'd hit me in the stomach. He wanted to teach me to fight back and to be tough because there would be situations in life and sports that you would have to display that."

You have to fight back in sports. You have to be a family. You have to reach out. It always comes back to family, and that is why Joe's kids are at the Stadium.

"They think it's all play, but I've learned from my father to be successful, and you have to put in long hours sometimes," Girardi said. "Your No. 1 job as the father is to provide for your family, and that's what he did. He took me everywhere. And wherever he went, I was right behind him and sometimes when he stopped, I ran into him."

That three-game series against the Cubs gave Girardi the chance to spend precious time with his dad in the middle of the baseball season. Jerry's son who used to play at Wrigley Field was now managing at Wrigley Field, and you can be sure Joe was thinking of his father those days in the visiting dugout at Wrigley when the Yankees lost the first game but came back to win the final two games of the series.

"It's really important because he is at the ending stages of Alzheimer's," Girardi explained on his show about seeing his dad. "My father is 80 years old and has probably had it for 16 or 17 years. He doesn't talk anymore. He doesn't get up. He can't walk. His eyes are closed all the time. Every time I get a chance to see him, I don't know if that is going to be the last time."

Just as his father taught him about the virtues of hard work, Girardi has passed those lessons along to his kids with Kim's help. "It's important your kids understand you work hard, I think it's important that the kids understand the importance of education, which my mother preached, which Kim preaches all the time to our kids," Girardi said. "I want my kids to work hard. I want them to earn what they get."

Earn what you get. Work for it. That's why Girardi is out there throwing batting practice to Dante or coaching him in youth football. The lessons never stop.

When Joe was a student at Northwestern, before classes began each year, Jerry would take Joe to a high school baseball field near the family restaurant, Washington High School, and feed balls into the pitching machine. There was always more work to be done. Joe would take 150 swings a day and one day he ripped a line drive right back at the machine and caught his father on the finger with the smash. And just like the day when he injured his thumb working on the bathtub faucet, Jerry didn't slow down one bit despite the mangled finger. "He never stopped working," Girardi told Curry. "But he got me back. And that was the thing about my father, he showed me that he was still in charge and was still tough. He spun a ball in the machine, and it actually hit me, and he said, 'Now, we're even.'"

The reality is that father and son never will be even. Joe cannot repay what his dad and mom did for him. In 1997, during an emotional Northwestern Athletic Hall of Fame induction, Girardi spoke for about 20 minutes at the Allen Center and had to compose himself every time he mentioned his mother, who had passed away many years earlier. He made sure to thank all of his family in the heartrending speech, pointing out how Kim used to pitch rolled up socks at him when they were first married. The highlight of the night, though, came when he talked about his dad. Then he took off his World Series ring that he had earned in 1996 with that dramatic triple against Greg Maddux and the Braves. He surprised his dad by giving him the ring. Later, he told *Northwestern Perspective*, "He deserves it. I wanted him to know that everything he did for me and all those years did not go unnoticed."

Soon after the event, Jerry relived the emotional night, telling the magazine, "Joe said, 'Dad, would you come up here. I've got something for you.' Well, I just choked up. I couldn't say a word. I gave him a big bear hug, and he gave me one. I had tears coming down like someone poured a bucket of water over my head."

Joe says his dad wore that ring every day up until about 2007, when he just became too sick to have the ring. Recalling that night now when he presented his dad with the 1996 World Series ring, Joe added, "It was extremely emotional for me because I think about all that my dad had invested in my life. There is no way that I would be where I am today if it wasn't for all the time that my father had put in my life raising me as a son, and not just a son, but as a son who knew how to fight for things he wanted, a son who knew how to work hard. Those are the things that he instilled in me. He instilled in me the toughness and the ability to go on maybe when you didn't feel your best."

He knows this essential truth about the game: "Baseball has a way of balancing itself out." So does life. Fight through the pain, fight through the adversity, and do the best job you can do, just like that day when Jerry Girardi fractured his thumb working on the bathtub faucet. Tape it up and move forward.

As for his four World Series rings, Girardi said all of them remain family rings. "I always tell my kids they are for them, so eventually I will pass them onto them," he said.

There just may be more World Series rings in Joe Girardi's future.

2.

FAMILY FIRST

WITH THE LINEUP posted, the color-coded binder in place, Joe Girardi was ready to manage another game for the New York Yankees and was set to take his usual place in the dugout.

"I feel like I am always at this rail," Girardi confided one day late in the 2011 season. "You never leave the rail. You are always standing in the dugout."

For Girardi, managing is much more than being seen as an isolated figure shown on television standing near the top step of the dugout. He wants life at the rail to stand for so much more.

Girardi rarely shows his inner self to the public and the New York baseball media. Look closely, though, and you see a different side of Girardi emerging. The 2012 season will be his fifth season as manager of the Yankees. He is signed through next season and expects to be here a lot longer.

World championships are always the goal in New York; make no mistake about that, but Girardi wants the Yankees to stand for more than titles. He wants the players to experience victory with a much deeper meaning. Everywhere Girardi played baseball, it was more than a game; it was a coming together of coaches and players.

Baseball is family. Baseball was the game that he believes helped keep his mother, Angela, alive for another six years after she was diagnosed with ovarian cancer and given only three months to live when Joe was 13. It was the game that bonded father and son on trips through the Midwest, the greatest of days, listening to Cubs games. Jerry Girardi has long suffered from Alzheimer's, and those baseball memories mean so much more to Joe now.

Baseball is having his wife, Kim, and their three children, Serena, Dante, and Lena, at the game and encouraging his players to bring their families to the ballpark and see baseball through a wider lens.

Baseball is a game. Girardi wants to make it family, too. Girardi wants the Yankees to think about championships in a family way. That's why he instituted a family day that is much more like a carnival, where there are activities for everyone in the family.

"I want the families around the ballpark," Girardi explained. "I want the kids to know what their fathers do for a living. My dad used to take me to work, and it's something that I will never forget, something I will cherish for the rest of my life. These are the moments you live for as a parent."

It's not just about the big money or the championships.

GM Brian Cashman said there are many special qualities to Girardi.

"He cares. He's got a big heart," noted Cashman, who hired Girardi the day before Halloween in 2007. "He works hard. He cares a great deal for everyone in here. He is sincerely trying to do everything in his power to accomplish everything together because he cares about what other people feel and think, and that's, I think, a strength.

"He was a quality leader as a player," Cashman added. "He was a quality leader as a coach. My expectation was that he would be the same as a manager. Until you are in that chair, it's a different experience."

Cashman admitted that the general public does not really understand Girardi.

"Probably not, because he has the crew-cut and stuff, he looks like, 'You're in the Army now.' That, I think, hides the fact that this is a deeply religious, caring, big-hearted person, who has discipline and structure, but he also has a big heart at the same time. You can have all of it. You can be disciplined and structured and have a huge heart, you can have that. But looks can be deceiving, and that probably plays into a little bit."

Flash back to that hot August day in the Bronx when the Yankees held Family Day. For the third straight game, Mariano Rivera struggled, this time surrendering a ninth-inning, three-run pinch-hit home run to Angels pinch-hitter Russell Branyan as the Yankees held on for a 6–5 victory. Doubts were beginning to creep in about age finally catching up to the greatest closer of all-time. Even baseball gods show their age.

One hour after the game had ended, though, there was the Great Rivera back on the field at Yankee Stadium, smiling and pitching once again, this time tossing Wiffle balls to his son as the scene around him unfolded as Yankee Stadium turned into your typical church carnival. He did not have a care in the world. No one lets go of a game quicker than Mariano Rivera. Girardi came out to talk and laugh with his closer.

This was a day of family, food, face-painting, and different play stations spread along the field set up for family enjoyment. Players who were not married had their girlfriends with them, casually strolling through the grounds as if they were in Central Park. Players mingled, superstars and bench players—this is all part of the way Girardi runs his club.

The Yankees trade players and every year make new signings, always with the idea of bettering the team—that is the way they do business. But Girardi is doing the best he can to make it more than the business of baseball for his players and those who work for the club. He is trying to build character, as well.

This is life with the Yankees under Joe Girardi. It's not just about the game. It's about making managing the New York Yankees much more a human experience than it seems to be to the casual observer, much more than just life along the rail.

On that Family Day, Girardi made it clear he was not about to lose one ounce of faith in Rivera, saying that he would only begin to doubt his legendary closer if "it happened for a month," not just three games. In a rare postgame address to the media, Girardi, who is extremely guarded with his words during pre- and postgame interviews, added, "I don't think Mo has forgotten how to pitch."

His message was clear. Don't quit on Rivera. And his faith was rewarded.

After surrendering that home run to Branyan, Rivera returned to his Hall of Fame self and went on to retire 17 straight batters from August 11 to August 29. By the end of the season, Rivera had compiled 44 saves to become the all-time saves leader with 603. You have to go back to 2004 to find a season where Rivera earned more saves (53). He recorded his 600th save in a September 13 win in Seattle, throwing a scoreless ninth inning. He became baseball's all-time saves leader six days later at home against the Twins, notching his 602nd save, surpassing Trevor Hoffman.

It was done in typical Rivera style, a 1-2-3 ninth inning, the 208th time in his career he gathered such a save, according to STATS. That save came 15 years and 125 days after his first save. He enters the 2012 season with one great pitch—a cutter—and 603 saves. He is 42 years old. He wears No. 42, the last player to wear the number that is retired throughout baseball as a tribute to Jackie Robinson. He owns 42 career postseason saves, also a record. Eleven of those saves have come in the World Series.

No, Mo had not forgotten how to pitch. When Girardi thinks of Rivera, he thinks back to the first time he saw a skinny kid on the mound.

"What comes to mind is 1996 when I got here," said Girardi, who caught 15 years in the major leagues, four with the Yankees during the amazing championship run under Joe Torre. "I got the chance to catch him in the bullpen, and I said, 'Who is this kid?' His stuff was electric. He was throwing 97. He was throwing wherever he wanted to. His stuff was cutting. He could elevate. And I never even heard of him. I had been a National Leaguer my whole career. I get traded over here in the fall of 1995, and I'm like, 'Man, this kid is special.' He kind of broke in slowly until all of a sudden he was going 2–2⅔ innings, shutting clubs down, the game seemed to be over early. If they didn't get to us by the sixth, the game was over. He was just so impressive."

Rivera has done all this with essentially one pitch—the cutter.

"It just shows you how great he is at his trade because he never really fooled people," Girardi said. "It wasn't like you were looking for a fastball and you get a change-up, or you're looking for a fastball and you get a curveball. Mo has said, 'Here it is. It's going to cut. It's going to sink, and I'm going to throw where I want. Try to do something with it.' I can't think of any pitcher who's really ever done that."

On this August day, the Yankees mustered enough firepower to win, thanks in part to Curtis Granderson's sky-high two-run home run, his 32nd of the season. Granderson has the perfect swing for the short right-field porch at Yankee Stadium. Under the patience of Girardi and the tutelage of hitting coach Kevin Long, Granderson began to blossom in the middle of the 2010 season and now is one of the most explosive hitters in the game. He finished his second year with the Yankees with a career-high 41 home runs, a career-high 119 RBIs, and 136 runs scored. He also has the perfect personality for New York, often out in the community, doing the most he can to help others.

As superstars like Derek Jeter and Alex Rodriguez age, Granderson and Robinson Cano provide a one-two punch for Girardi that should keep the Yankees in the postseason for years to come.

Girardi has done many things other than change his uniform number since taking over as manager in 2008. When he got the job, the first thing he did was put the No. 27 on his back to show that he was willing to carry the weight of pinstripe expectations for a record 27th championship.

It's as if Girardi were saying, "Put it on me, I can handle it. Bring it on. This is who we are as a team."

He might as well have painted a bull's-eye on his back. But that is another part of the Girardi experience. He is not afraid to take the heat for his players to put them in a more relaxed state of mind. And he'll even make a joke at his own expense.

Granderson, who reached 105 runs scored and 93 RBIs in that 6–5 win over the Angels, on his way to an MVP-like year, had started the season batting either eighth or ninth in 10 of the Yankees' first 13 games in Girardi's lineup.

When that point was brought to Girardi's attention, he said with a laugh, "What was I thinking?" You can be sure of one thing, Joe Girardi is always thinking.

"I call Joe 'Mr. Speedy,'" said Tony Pena, his bench coach, a former major league manager, and, like Girardi, a former catcher. "He's always got somewhere to go or is thinking of what to do next. That's Joe. That's who he is. He never stops."

And yes, one championship is not nearly enough. In the last 17 years the Yankees have been to the postseason 16 times, winning five World Series.

In 2009 the Yankees christened the new Yankee Stadium with their 27th world championship with Girardi doing a masterful job of making the most of his weapons, even going to a three-man rotation in October to get the most out of his ace, CC Sabathia, the always enigmatic A.J. Burnett, and veteran lefty Andy Pettitte, and allowing veterans Johnny Damon and Hideki Matsui, who would both soon be former Yankees, to play fearless baseball in the six-game victory over the Phillies in the World Series.

The Yankees had not won a world championship since 2000 under Joe Torre. Torre's Yankees had won four world championships with Girardi the catcher on hand for three of those titles. Girardi delivered in a big way in so many ways. His third-inning triple in Game 6 of the 1996 World Series against the Braves and Greg Maddux remains a glorious moment in Yankees history and helped kick-start that dynasty.

"He was not known for his hitting, but that was probably the biggest hit that got this dynasty going," former first baseman Tino Martinez said of Girardi's triple.

Martinez has watched the evolution of Joe Girardi the manager. There is much more to Girardi than the TV camera shows. Most of all, there is the thought process of taking care of everyone in the Yankees family, and that casts a wide net. Martinez recognizes that as only a caring teammate would, having known Girardi since 1996 when they both showed up to play for the Yankees, Martinez coming from Seattle, Girardi arriving from Colorado.

"That's why Joe is a great manager, he's worried about everybody," Martinez explained. "He's worried about the guy on the bench who is not playing that day. He wants everybody to do well.

That year, 1996, he became a leader on the field and in the clubhouse. He took control of the staff. We weren't expected to do much as a team. He didn't care about his hitting. If he struck out four times, he cared only about his pitcher. He wanted to call a great game. All he was concerned about was the wins and losses. He wasn't worried about his average or how many guys he threw out, it was all about winning, and he was happy."

Quickly and quietly in 1996, Girardi became the leader that Torre said he could lean on, and that kind of leadership rubbed off on the rest of the team. Remember, Jeter was only in his first full season as a Yankee in 1996 and was not ready to take charge of such a team.

Girardi left the Yankees after the 1999 season and the Yankees' four-game sweep of the Braves, signing back with his beloved Cubs as a free agent for his second stint in Chicago. Jorge Posada was now the Yankees' everyday catcher. In his 15 years, Girardi played for the Cubs twice for a total of seven seasons, the expansion Rockies for three seasons, four years with the Yankees and a final season with the Cardinals in 2003, watching and learning the entire time. He played for such respected managers as Don Zimmer, Don Baylor, Torre, and Tony LaRussa.

"I got to play in, you could argue, three of the top baseball cities in the world in Chicago, St. Louis, and New York, and got to play for an expansion team that drew over 4 million fans three years in a row," Girardi said with wonder of his playing career. "Those were special times."

Girardi, though, was always hard on himself as a player. He always expected more out of himself, admitting of his long playing career, "There were some long sleepless nights."

When his playing career ended, he followed the advice of his wife, Kim, who has always sees the best in Joe and where he best fits as a player and a person. He could have gone into some team's front office or made a lucrative career in broadcasting, but she knew he had what it took to be a successful major league manager, so that was the goal he pursued, landing his first managerial job with the Marlins in 2006.

Girardi readily acknowledges that Kim is the one who is not afraid to take risks and that he leans to the more conservative side. In that respect, he said, "We're total opposites."

After the Yankees came so close to winning another World Series in 2001 under Torre, losing Game 7 to the Diamondbacks on Luis Gonzalez's single over a drawn-in infield, the Yankees lost again two years later in 2003 to Jack McKeon's Magical Marlins. Times were changing.

The next season the face of the AL East changed dramatically. It was the Red Sox who became the Beast of the East. The Yankees blew a 3–0 ALCS lead to the Red Sox in 2004, and things were never the same. The long Torre marriage ended after the 2007 season. The Yankees, and Torre, needed a change.

It became Girardi's job in 2008 to get these Yankees to buy into the team concept, and that first year the Yankees did not make it to the postseason for the first time since the strike-shortened season of 1994. But the seeds of a championship were planted in 2008, and by 2009, the first year of the new Yankee Stadium, Girardi guided the Yankees to title No. 27.

When you live life along the rail, you are always looking ahead. Girardi immediately switched to uniform No. 28. The game is never about yesterday for Girardi, it's always about tomorrow.

The Yankees remain a team in transition, still determined to win world championships, but trying to do it with a little different model. Older parts are being replaced by Cashman, and it's up to Girardi to fit the new parts into a winning machine with young players like Brett Gardner and a pitching staff that includes Michael Pineda, Ivan Nova, and David Robertson.

The transition included Russell Martin replacing Jorge Posada behind the plate. Girardi knows all about the perspective of being an aging catcher. It was Posada who replaced Girardi. The game is constantly changing.

The 2011 season once again showed how unpredictable October can be as the St. Louis Cardinals, who won the NL wild-card in wild comeback fashion, went on to win the World Series, first beating the highly favored Phillies in the NLDS, then the Brewers to win the National League pennant and topping the Texas Rangers by winning Games 6 and 7 to win it all for LaRussa.

Twice in Game 6 LaRussa's Cardinals were down to their last strike, but came back to win. Just before the World Series started, Texas president Nolan Ryan proved to be a fortune teller when he said watching his team in the playoffs was like riding "the Texas Giant at Six Flags, the roller coaster. You can go from the top to the bottom real quick at times."

The same could be said for the Yankees.

The Yankees have come up short the last two seasons, losing in the ALCS to the Rangers in 2010 and being stunned by the Tigers in the deciding Game 5 of the 2011 ALDS when one big hit would have made the difference. Despite those losses, Girardi believes the Yankees have the talent to win a championship. The goal never changes.

"I feel good about this team," Girardi said, looking ahead to the 2012 season. "I was extremely proud of the way we overcame a lot of things and the way our young kids stepped up. And these kids are going to be better because they have another year under their belt, and I have a feeling there are going to be more kids who are going to step up, and we need that because we have players that have some age. They are not going to be there forever, and somebody has to step up, and our guys have done a good job.

"The one thing that I think is important for a manager is that the players know that you care but also never forget how hard it is to play the game," Girardi explained. "The effort is there all the time, but sometimes it just doesn't happen. Some days a guy gets three hits, and he's going to take the same approach the next day. It just doesn't happen, and that's why there is the human element of the game."

Make no mistake. With the Yankees, life is still all about winning world championships. But Girardi is trying to guide the Yankees in a different manner, making it more of a family atmosphere, not the Evil Empire the Yankees have been depicted by Red Sox president Larry Lucchino, who has put the heat on the Yankees by hiring former Mets manager Bobby Valentine as Red Sox manager after the September collapse shook up the Red Sox's world. The Red Sox's battles against the Yankees will once again be the focus of the AL East. Valentine will be explosive in the way he manages and in taking on the Yankees, saying the day he got hired, "I think we are going to be able to match them."

Lucchino said he wants Valentine to "poke the bear" that is the Yankees. Valentine will be center stage with the Boston media, an entertaining lot. Girardi often acts in a way that turns off much of the media in the media capital of the world. With the new Yankee Stadium has come new rules, less openness to the media, and there have been rough patches with aging Yankees stars like Posada, but Girardi has made it clear that the Yankees are his family. You protect and take care of your family.

The days of the Bronx Zoo are long gone. New players are welcomed. They all stir the drink.

"I think our club has done a good job of when guys have come up," Girardi noted. "They'd made them fit in because we've had a number of people who have had to help us, more on the pitching staff than anywhere else. They've made guys feel welcome, they've made them feel like they are a part of this, that they are going to play a big role, and they have.

"The first thing I tell them is you are going to be a part of this, I tell each player how I am going to use them, I talk to all the relievers about how I use relievers here, that I am not going to abuse you. That your families are welcome; I want to see your kids around, all of that because I think that is important."

In the end, staying together as a team is what matters most and is what makes winning possible in New York these days. The names will continue to change, but Girardi believes that if the Yankees take that family approach to their jobs, they will succeed.

There is more organization than in the past. Girardi has made the most of information age. There is the infamous color-coded Girardi Binder, packed full of match-ups and Yankees scouting and the team's computer secrets. The former engineering student Girardi approaches managing decisions on a day-to-day level as a process. There is a reason for everything. There are parameters. There is thinking behind every decision and numbers that weigh in all of Girardi's calculations. Mr. Speedy is always thinking ahead.

Torre was a tremendous role model for Girardi, but Girardi is running the Yankees his own way. He is using his binder and his color-coded charts. The combination of brain power and heart is what his new Yankees are all about.

"You're covering so many more bases than as a coach," says Girardi, who was Torre's bench coach in 2005, getting a taste of what the New York managing story is all about. "I never talked about the roster when I was a player. I never had to worry about who my starters were, that was all Joe's department. So it's just so much different. Yes, as a catcher, you worry about the other guys, but really, like any player, you really worry about yourself, making sure that you are prepared. Not making sure that everyone else is prepared."

Now Girardi has to make sure everyone is prepared.

And, in the end, despite all that preparation, if the Yankees don't get the big hit, they can wind up being knocked out of the first round of the playoffs like they were by the Tigers in the 2011 ALDS, losing at home in the final game, 3–2.

It can end too soon, no matter what. It can end with the team going 1-for-9 with runners in scoring position in that final game. The binder isn't foolproof.

Girardi, 47, is built like a rock, he works out every day. His family is the center of his universe. Often after a game, win or lose, Girardi will be in right field throwing batting practice to Dante. The shouts of excitement of a father enjoying the accomplishments of the son echo throughout a silent Yankee Stadium, and when Dante reaches the seats with a swing, there is the same kind of cheer you would hear from a father at a Little League game.

The Yankees could suffer a crushing loss or the most inspirational win, and 45 minutes after a game, Girardi is throwing a bucket of baseballs to Dante in the green cathedral that is Yankee Stadium. Lessons are learned on that field every day, but it is about the bigger experience. The game is about family. That's always the way it has been in Girardi's life.

That's the way Joe Girardi was raised in East Peoria, Illinois.

3.

THE PLAN

LIFE IS NEVER a straight path. There are twists and turns along the way. No matter how much you try to plan your life, it rarely goes the way that you draw it up.

In 1987, at Class A Winston-Salem, Joe Girardi lost his passion for baseball and walked away from the game for a short time. Looking at Girardi now and seeing his square jaw and his passion for baseball and for life, it's hard to imagine him walking away from anything.

In his heart, though, Joe, at the age of 22, had to figure out why he was playing professional baseball. For years he had convinced himself that he was playing the game to help keep his mother alive. That is a heavy burden, but at the same time, that gave him a sense of purpose to his game. It made him play each play with passion. Girardi is always concerned about others. That is what defines him as a person, as a father, as a husband, and as a player and manager. As a catcher, he was always there for his pitcher. As a manager, he is always there for his players. As a father and a husband, he is always there for his family.

After his mother, Angela, was diagnosed with ovarian cancer when Joe was 13, he convinced himself that he was playing the game for her. Baseball was helping to keep her alive. It gave her hope. Angela was given only three to six months to live and defied all odds by living six more years. During that time she got to watch Joe blossom as a baseball player and a young man.

"She was a fighter," Joe said.

In the summer of his junior season at Northwestern University, she finally lost the battle and passed away.

Joe stayed with the game, graduated, and was drafted by his hometown Cubs in the fifth round of the 1986 draft. That summer he was able to stay home and play in Peoria for the Cubs Class A team and spend so much time with his dad, a unique situation for any minor league player. It was a wonderful experience for Joe and his father, a lifelong Cubs fan, who passed his love for the Cubs to his son.

The next season, Joe was sent to Winston-Salem. Far away from home, Girardi began to lose the passion for the game he so loved, the game that sustained him. One day he just walked away and went back home to Peoria. Suddenly, all of his life's plans were up in the air.

"I walked away from the game just because I didn't understand why I was playing," Girardi said of that critical time in his life. "I didn't know what my hope was in. I walked away for a week."

By walking away from baseball, though, Girardi found himself and realized there was a much bigger plan to his life. His girlfriend, Kim, who would become his wife two years later, helped Joe realize why he was playing baseball. Kim told him he had been given a gift from God, and she told Joe that it was up to him to make the most of that gift. Instead of walking away from baseball, walk toward it, embrace the game once again. Baseball could help open doors to help others.

In a word, baseball offered hope.

"That was the one thing that Kim helped me realize, that there was hope and that I would get through this," Girardi said. "That's when I became a Christian. Kim made me realize that God had given me a gift. That's why I was playing. I used to think that I was playing to give my mom something to live for."

Joe gave his mom much to live for by playing baseball and by being a good son. When she died, that was not the end of the road for his career; that was only the beginning, and hope would go on to show itself in so many ways. "My mom passed in 1984 when she was 48," Girardi said. A quarter of a century later, her final words to him still resonate. "She said, 'Don't forget me,' and I never have," Joe explained. Those final three words are the most powerful words in Joe's life.

"For me, it just left such a lasting impression," he explained, "and I think what it does, is it always makes me think about what I am doing in my life because my mom was really giving about giving up her time in helping others. She was a pet lover, where she would adopt every stray. She had a love for God's creations, and it makes me think about what I'm doing all the time."

Angela Girardi was all about hope. Baseball was a game to be enjoyed and to be cherished. Every single pitch was to be cherished. Honor the game. Honor your mother. Honor your life. And honor your gift. Be the best that you can be, and honor God's gift. In baseball, there is always hope.

Kim's words hit home and made all the difference. Angela's final words pushed Joe forward and became his guiding light. His place in the game made sense to Joe. From that point on in his career, Joe Girardi never looked back, only forward, and his faith has been rewarded in so many ways. In two short years following his conversation with Kim, he was in the majors playing for the Cubs.

As his career developed, he was able to help others in so many ways as he was able to start his own charity, called Catch 25. Ten years into his major league career, his father became a victim of Alzheimer's. "Our charity has taken a while to formulate what is in our hearts," Girardi explained. "Originally, it was to donate money for research on Alzheimer's and cancer because I lost my mom to cancer, Kim lost her sister. My father is struggling with Alzheimer's. But what we realized is wanted to broaden it, and make it a foundation based on giving people hope."

For Girardi, it all comes back to having hope; no situation is too dark to not have hope.

"What I've seen in my life is the importance of hope," Girardi said. "My mom had hope that she was going to get better, that there were certain things in her life that she wanted to see before she passed. This was a woman who was given three to six months to live, but I think the hope that she had brought her to live six years. And what I see through the devastation of cancer and watching what Kim's sister went through, people need hope. When people pass, their siblings or their children need hope. We believe that things are going to be okay and that they are going to get through this."

There is always hope. It comes down to how Girardi was raised by his mom and dad and the values that Kim and Joe have passed on to their three children, Serena, Dante, and Lena. It is about how you live your life each day. It can show itself in so many ways, in leadership, in helping teammates, in helping others. As it turned out, baseball, just as Kim said, would give Joe the platform to make a difference.

As manager of the Yankees, Girardi's team won the world championship in only his second year on the job in 2009. On the night the Yankees won the title, the night Mariano Rivera threw the final pitch to secure world championship No. 27 for the Yankees with a 7–3 victory over the Philadelphia Phillies, Girardi reached another one of his life's goals. He won three world championships as a player with the Yankees and now had won a championship with the Yankees as manager, all in the space of 14 seasons; an amazing accomplishment and something that Girardi could never have dreamed of when he walked away from baseball that week in 1987. Back then he was a Cub, never knowing that his life would become so intertwined with New York. His mother's words have stayed with him all that time. "Don't forget me."

On the special night that you reach one of your life's goals, if you happen to pass a motorist in danger on the way home after the biggest victory of your managerial life, you make sure you stop and help that person. That's exactly what Girardi did.

"It was about 2:00 o'clock in the morning, and I had my kids in the car, who were both recovering from the flu that they got in Philadelphia," Girardi said of that November night the Yankees won the World Series. "We were driving along and we saw the car, and Kim said, 'Stop, you got to stop.' So I stopped and ran across the street. A lady had hit the inside wall of where the Cross-County turns into the Hutch.

"The car was pretty mangled when I went over there. She was okay, but I was afraid because a window had been broken, she had glass all over her lap, and of course, she was a little frantic. My concern was getting her out of the car because she was on a corner, and I didn't want someone to come along and hit her from behind. Fortunately, the police got there pretty quickly. Kim had called 911."

That's a pretty full day, winning a World Series and helping out a motorist in distress, but it is all part of life. You can't plan that. Situations arise and you respond. When you are called, you answer, you help, and you offer hope.

You also can't plan your next trip to the World Series. It doesn't just happen that way.

Girardi looks back on that 2009 team, which included veterans Johnny Damon and Hideki Matsui, and said of all those Yankees, "Those guys played so hard and they played smart. You think about the smart play by Johnny. How resilient we were. In [the ALCS] we lost a tough game out in Anaheim, and they bounced back. Those are the things I think about."

In that ALCS the Yankees lost Game 5 in Anaheim 7–6 to the Angels and came back to the Bronx and the new Yankee Stadium to close out the series and move on to the World Series with a 5–2 win over Mike Scioscia's club. Andy Pettitte got the clinching victory just as he did in every postseason series that year, and in each of those games Mariano Rivera got the final out.

In the clinching Game 6 of the World Series, Matsui homered and doubled and drove in six runs against the Phillies, and that smart play by Johnny Damon that Girardi mentioned was a "double steal" on the same pitch in Game 4 at Citizens Bank Park in the Yankees 7–4 victory. This was an amazing heads-up play. The game was tied at 4–4 going into the ninth as the Phillies were trying to even the World Series at two wins apiece. After getting a two-out single in a nine-pitch at-bat against Phillies closer Brad Lidge, Damon was off and running. With the drastic infield shift on against Mark Teixeira, who was batting left-handed, Damon stole second base and bounced up and continued to third because third baseman Pedro Feliz took the throw at second. The off-line throw carried Feliz toward the first-base side of second, giving Damon his opening, and he did not hesitate. Damon dashed to third, which was not covered by any Phillies fielder.

Teixeira was then hit by a pitch, putting runners at first and third. Alex Rodriguez, who had a monster postseason, drove home Damon with a double, and Jorge Posada knocked in two runs with a single. That victory gave the Yankees a 3–1 lead in the World Series.

It all came back to Damon's "double steal." As Damon came up from his slide at second base, he just took off, beating Feliz to the bag at third. It was a play of daring and creative ingenuity by

Damon, a play that could not be scripted. Feliz said after the game, "He saw nobody on the other side and took off."

"I'm just glad that when I started running, I still had my young legs behind me," Damon said, adding, "I think Joe probably remembers those Kansas City days. I just went off instinct, and fortunately, it worked out."

Sometimes it works out in the postseason, sometimes it doesn't.

In each of the next two postseasons, Girardi's Yankees did not make it back to the World Series. In 2010 the Texas Rangers beat them in six games in the ALCS. In 2011, after posting the best record in the American League and gaining home-field advantage throughout the AL playoffs, the Yankees lost the deciding Game 5 at Yankee Stadium to the Detroit Tigers in the ALDS.

The Yankees worked all season for that home-field advantage and wound up losing two of three games at home to the Tigers in the series, scoring only two runs in that final game and three runs in the 5–3 Game 2 loss. During the regular season the Yankees spent 98 days in first place. At Yankee Stadium they posted a 52–29 record, averaging 5.8 runs per game during the season, yet in those two losses at home in the postseason, the Yankees scored a total of five runs.

Sometimes, you don't get the big hit, and in a blink of an eye the season can end.

"You realize how tough it is," Girardi said of the lessons learned in the last two postseasons. "That's the one thing you realize, how difficult it is to win a World Series. There are so many things that have to happen. You start in spring training, you play 30 games there, you play 162 games in the regular season, and it is difficult when it ends so abruptly because any team that gets in the playoffs really believes they can win the World Series. I think you can play the same eight teams, and I don't think the same team is going to win. You'd have a different winner if you did it again. It's just the way the game is."

There are twists and turns along the way. It rarely goes the way you draw it up.

The St. Louis Cardinals came from nowhere to win the NL wild-card in 2011 and went on to win the World Series, even though they were twice down to their last strike in Game 6 and had to win Games 6 and 7 to prevail. The Cardinals were the last team that Girardi played for in his career in 2003. Though the Yankees didn't make it to the World Series, Girardi was happy for St. Louis manager Tony LaRussa, an old friend.

"I learned a lot from Tony," Girardi said. "I appreciate Tony LaRussa so much more once I became a manager. I really did. Any time I got a chance to pick his brain, I always picked it, and he was great about it. He would even come up to me and present different situations to me. He would say, 'I know you want to manage in the future. What do you think about this situation?' He would do that, and I loved it. I've been blessed to play for all the managers I've played for."

The Big Four during his 15-year player career were Don Zimmer, in his first go-round with the Cubs; Don Baylor in Colorado and during Girardi's second stint with the Cubs; Joe Torre in New York; and then LaRussa the final year of Girardi's playing career.

"I know God planned it a lot better than I planned it," Girardi said of the way his playing career went and the cities he played in during those 15 years. Life rarely goes the way you draw it up. When Girardi was drafted by the hometown Cubs, he thought he would spend his entire playing career in Chicago, especially after going to the playoffs his first season in Chicago in 1989.

He also had no idea that his major league career would last 15 years.

"It's not how I would have drawn it up," Girardi said. "When you grow up and your first love is the Chicago Cubs, and you're playing for the Cubs and you win the first year that you play for them, you're in the playoffs: A) You think you are going to be in the playoffs every year, and B) you think you are going to be a Cub the rest of your life.

"How did I know that my life would take me to Colorado, which was a tremendous stop, very enjoyable, and then to New York, which was great, back to Chicago, and then to play a year in St. Louis and to think about that I grew up playing Cubs vs. Cardinals? I grew up halfway between each city, and I got the chance to play for all those great franchises."

For Girardi, it all comes down to faith, no matter what the challenge or the twists and turns of life that come about. "I think faith is a way of life," he explained. "When I think about my career path and what I've done, I believe I've been able to do everything in my life because I've been extremely blessed by God. This is not something that I've done. I've been blessed."

That is the way he looks at his life. In a way, it is a similar approach that Denver Broncos quarterback Tim Tebow has in his life. Tebow has his many critics, but he took the NFL by storm in 2011, even becoming a *Sports Illustrated* cover boy.

Girardi, who loves football and was a high school quarterback, has followed the Tebow story and said this of the QB: "I think he is a man who has convictions, who has extremely strong faith. He is extremely humble and has the will to win. What I see in Tim Tebow is that he makes people better around him. I think his teammates see he walks the walk, he's not just words. What he talks about, he walks, so I think they respect it. They may not all believe the same way that he believes, but I think they all respect him. I think they see how hard he plays, too, and that he has no regards for his body, he just plays hard."

That's exactly how Girardi played baseball.

"I always felt that I'd be protected and that you feel that the preparation you do will physically protect you," Girardi of his hard-nosed style of play. "That was the only way I knew how to play, and that came from the way my parents raised me."

For Joe, it always comes back to his parents. He was raised right by Angela and Jerry. "I always thought my parents were there for me, and they always walked through things with me. Whether I was going through good things or tough things, I could always count on them."

Those life's lessons remain with Girardi to this day, and when his daughter, Serena, had to wear braces a few years ago, Joe had braces put on his teeth, as well. Yes, he needed some dental work, but he could have lived without it, this is the point he was making to Serena: "I just felt, if Daddy could do it, you could do it too," he said.

Faith works in many ways for Girardi, and after he came to the realization that baseball was a calling as much as a game; it gave him a sense of relief as a player and it continues to this day. "Faith, it also relieves your mind in so many ways," he said. "I believe it is God's plan. So wherever I end up, it's not my doing. I don't need to put too much pressure on what I'm going to be five years from now or 10 years from now because God is going to put me there. So to me, I'm following His plan. As humans we like to plan it out, but I think you can ask any person and I think they will tell you that their life has not gone exactly as they thought it would go. My life did not go exactly as I thought it would go. I didn't think that I would be managing the Yankees this quickly. I never imagined playing for the Yankees. I think all the positive things that have happened in my life because I played for the Yankees, it's unbelievable."

All from a game he was going to walk away from if not for the eye- and heart-opening comments from Kim. And Girardi walks the walk about not worrying about where he will wind up in five years. That's what helped carry him through his experience as manager of the Florida Marlins.

Girardi's first managerial stop was in Florida in 2006 after spending the previous season as Torre's bench coach with the Yankees. A young manager was getting the opportunity of a lifetime with a young team, and Girardi made the most of the Marlins' low payroll. That season the Marlins' total payroll was $14,998,834, according to the website Cot's Baseball Contracts. The Yankees payroll that season was $194 million. Girardi won the NL Manager of the Year Award in 2006, named both by the Baseball Writers' Association of America and the *Sporting News*. At the age of 41 he was the youngest manager in Marlins history.

He also wound up getting fired by Marlins owner Jeffrey Loria because of philosophical differences that stemmed from an incident in early August when Loria yelled at home plate umpire Larry Vanover and Girardi told his owner to stop yelling, that he had crossed a line. In the end, it all worked out the best for Girardi.

"I just think that was God's plan," Girardi said again, adding, "I wouldn't have drawn it up that way."

No, life is never a straight path.

Girardi has learned to make the most of every opportunity—even when the game is halted as it was by the last strike to hit the sport. In 1994 Girardi was heavily involved in the Major League Baseball Players Association during those most difficult labor times as the strike began on August 12 and lasted 232 days. MLBPA executive director Michael Weiner was the assistant general counsel at the time and worked closely with Girardi, who was a member of the negotiating committee, and all the players on the committee. Weiner was in the trenches with Girardi.

"That was the most difficult, the most intense fight that the union has had in its history," Weiner said. "Joe was one of the dozen or so guys on the front line. Joe always took his responsibilities to the union very, very seriously, both in terms of making sure for himself and his family that he understood what was at stake and what his rights were. That's what makes the union.

"Joe is very passionate and he's very earnest and he's very principled," Weiner said. "Even though he is open-minded and tolerant of other views, he has very little patience for the non-principled views. If somebody disagrees with Joe, he will work hard to figure out what the merit of that person's position is, but frequently, in that round of bargaining, there wasn't anything to find as to what was the basis of their position, other than, 'We just want to break the union,' or, 'We just want this,' or, 'We just want that.'

"Joe would struggle at times with the process because he had no patience for that. He had to learn, and he had a lot of great support from players like Scott Sanderson," Weiner explained. Joe was 29 at the time, Sanderson was 37. The right-handed pitcher, who pitched 19 years in the majors, compiling a 163–143 record, was a tremendous help to Girardi, helping to guide him through the fight.

"Scott has a different kind of personality and had the ability to try to explain to Joe that you've got to see this from a longer haul," Weiner said. "Joe worked hard and ultimately did develop patience for the process."

Girardi made the most of the difficult circumstances, and he put his engineering degree to good use, trying to gather as much information as possible each day. "Some players are impatient because they are impatient," Weiner said. "Some players are impatient because they say, 'Why can't we just get from here to there?' That wasn't it with Joe, it was just, 'I understand this is a process, I understand this is a negotiation, I understand you just can't put your best offer on the table, but why do we have to deal with dissembling, why do we have to deal with untruths, why do we have to deal with posturing, why do we have to deal with all this other stuff?'"

In the end the players stayed together, and Girardi was a big part of that. "Joe was one of the key guys," Weiner said, "one of the essential player leaders who devoted a tremendous amount of time and personal energy to the negotiations. The union would not be where it is without that group of guys who made an enormous contribution to that negotiation, and because of the nature of that negotiation, to all the successes the players have had since then."

That is some heady stuff, and today's players owe much to that group of players. Baseball is the one major sport today with a tremendous working relationship between players and owners, and it all goes back to those difficult days of 1994 to 1995.

On a personal level, Weiner noted, "You can't really have a conversation with Joe without him mentioning his family. Getting to work with guys like Joe Girardi is what makes working for the Players Association a great job because he has those principles and he's a great union member, but he also will challenge you. He's not afraid to challenge you to make sure what you are saying makes sense. He wants to make sure what you are saying is right, and I've always enjoyed that part of Joe. He was always incredibly respectful and courteous—that's part of his principles, as well—but that didn't mean that he wasn't going to ask you a question if he didn't understand something or challenge you if he thought you were wrong. You can't ask for anything more than that. He's going to challenge you to make sure you are doing your job to the best of your ability."

Getting the best out of those around him is what Girardi tries to do every day. He did that as a catcher for his pitchers, going all the way back to when he was in youth baseball and throughout his major league career. He does it as a manager with his players. All that success goes back to his faith and the way he was raised as a child and the many people who were there to help guide him throughout his blessed life.

4.

A BASEBALL HOME

SOMETIMES A POSITION finds you. Joe Girardi started out as an infielder. Then one day Girardi's travel ball coach, Dave Rodgers, had an idea. He wanted to switch Joe to catcher. He wanted his Sea Merchants to be led by Joe Girardi.

Joe didn't like the thought of switching positions, but he didn't complain to his coach. That's not in his makeup. The team comes first.

"He has such strong faith," Rodgers explained. "It's within him to lead by example. He was that way since he was 10 years old when I first started coaching him. That's always been Joe's way of doing things. He leads by example and never wavers.

"When I switched him to catcher, he didn't like it at all," Rodgers said. "I don't think my picture was on his refrigerator after I made that move. He knew he couldn't pitch or play infield when he caught. He never talked back to me. He just told his mother that he wanted to play third base and pitch. When my catcher went down, I knew Joe was the best catcher, and he went back there and caught ever since."

Girardi was 12 when he made the change.

"I wasn't happy with the switch," he explained.

He worked hard at his new position.

"It was my determination and my passion for the game that helped me succeed," he said. "And the work ethic that I saw at home, how to persevere. You didn't let anything bother you. You didn't let anything get in your way that really helped me. And I loved the strategy of the game."

Catching allowed Girardi to dig deeper into the strategy of baseball. The catcher is such a unique position. It is the only position in baseball where you face the other way, looking out at the entire field. The game is in your hands and in your head, and Girardi quickly took to his new position.

"He was a natural back there," Rodgers said. "He could throw from his knees. He did everything right back there."

Girardi eventually grew accustomed to the position.

"I didn't have to teach him a whole lot," Rodgers said. "He was the mainstay of that team."

Joe was small. When Joe first joined the team at the age of 10, he played outfield, and someone yelled to Rodgers, "Coach, you got a cap out in left field."

"It was Joe," Rodgers recalled with a laugh. "He wasn't even supposed to be on that team, but he was the best 10-year-old in the whole area, so I put him on the team. Then I moved him to third base, then catcher. He was the best athlete I had, and he was so tough."

When you see the Girardi crew cut, you get the impression that he always wore his hair that way. Short, like a Marine. But when Rodgers first met Joe, the youngster had long, curly locks of hair, much like Girardi's nine-year-old son, Dante, wears his hair these days, looking more like a surfer than someone in boot camp.

"Joe had that long, curly, sandy blond hair," Rodgers said.

When he was young, his father encouraged him to keep his hair short. "I had crew cuts for a long time, and then I let it grow out.

Then I went back to the crew cut. It's amazing how wise your father is," Joe said with a laugh.

Rodgers' travel team out of East Peoria, Illinois, was years ahead of its time. They also had a great name—the Sea Merchants—and a great team.

"The Sea Merchants were like rock-star idols around here because if you played for the Sea Merchants, you were good," Rodgers explained.

Joe loved playing for the Sea Merchants. "We played 50 games a summer from the time I was 10 years old," he said. "I think one year we ended up 48–2."

Rodgers used to call in the scores to the local paper, the same paper that Girardi delivered as a youngster, the *Peoria Journal Star*.

One time the reporter told Rodgers, "Coach, make sure you call in your losses, too."

Rodgers didn't miss a beat, saying, "We haven't lost yet."

Rodgers, a teacher, noted, "We didn't lose too many games when Joe was playing, a typical year was something like 54–6. Part of the reason why we were so good was that I was off all summer and we'd practice every day."

Preparation was drilled into Girardi's baseball soul at a young age. Joe's real passion was football, but being a catcher in baseball offered up some of the same qualities as football. You put on the catcher's gear, the shin guards, the chest protector, and the helmet. You also were able to strategize behind the plate.

His coach had a certain way of doing things. "I was pretty demanding back then," said Rodgers, who is 66. "If you get a base hit," he explained, "you better get to first base before the outfielder gets to the ball."

You also didn't swing at a 3–0 pitch.

One time Joe hit a home run on just such a 3–0 pitch.

"He came around third, and he wouldn't look at me," Rodgers said. "He had his head down and he wouldn't look at me. When I saw him in the dugout, I said to him, 'You know you're lucky. If that ball wouldn't have gone out of the ballpark, you would not be playing right now.' He got the drift. There were things that we just wouldn't compromise on. We tried to train them to be two-strike hitters so if you got two strikes you really have to work on fouling them off, stuff like that."

That is exactly the game plan of Girardi's Yankees. No team wears out pitchers like the Yankees consistently do. The goal every game is to get the starting pitcher into a high pitch count as early as possible. Dave Rodgers' teams were doing the exact same thing back in 1974.

Girardi's hitters take the same approach into the batter's box that he did 38 years ago.

"We were ahead of our time because we did demand that," Rodgers said. "A lot of people didn't like that. We told them this is the way it's got to be, and they did it."

Discipline became a lifestyle for the players. And it really wasn't about baseball, it was about much more. It was about life. Discipline is Girardi's calling card.

"And I'm glad of that," Rodgers said. "I just wanted those boys to become good men, good fathers, good husbands, and Joe has lived up to that. I don't care if he is the manager of the Yankees or not. He's a good father and a good husband, and that's what we told them after every loss.

"Nobody got hurt. Nobody got killed. And all you're trying to do is learn that you don't go home and kick the dog if things go wrong."

That was great advice. There was other advice.

Rodgers believed that air-conditioning was not good for a player. He thought it would make a body stiff and sore. So, on those sweltering Midwest nights, he convinced his players to have the air-conditioning turned off in their homes.

"Joe stayed in the same room as his brother, George," said Rodgers. "I had a rule you couldn't have air-conditioning on the day of the game. I didn't have my air-conditioning on, either. I suffered just like they did.

"His mother once said to me, 'You know how many days we went without air-conditioning?' I said, 'Oh, I'm sorry. I never thought about the ramifications to the rest of the family.' Joe was the one who took everything to heart and followed it religiously. If you said something, he believed it."

Did he ever.

Rodgers believed an arm had to be kept loose and warm to avoid injury so he recommended to his players that when they went to bed at night, they take an old tube sock, cut off the toe end, pull it up over your shoulder and wear that sock on your throwing arm, much like the Under Armour clothing line that players wear today.

"I just didn't want anybody stiff and sore," Rodgers recalled.

Joe made sure the air-conditioning was turned off, but he would put the fan on, and in this way he "protected" his arm. Young Joe believed in what his coach said, every word. He religiously followed Rodgers' advice and wore that sock on his arm, night after night.

"He wore it all the way through college," Rodgers said.

Many years later, Joe's wife, Kim, met Rodgers, "She grabbed my arm and told me, 'Would you please tell Joe that it's okay, he doesn't have to wear that sleeve anymore?'"

Joe had been wearing a sock on his arm for all those years to protect it.

Joe Girardi, though, never had a sore arm. And in Kim he found the perfect girl.

"I knew right away she was perfect for Joe, and I told her so because she put up with all the baseball stuff," Rodgers said.

"Joe always believed in his coaches, and if they told him stuff, he believed them," Rodgers said. "He just believes in human nature. He's a man of his world, and if somebody says something to them, and he believes in it, he's going to do it."

When you understand that about Girardi, other pieces of the puzzle begin to fall into place.

Consider a controversial play from the 2011 season when umpire Dana DeMuth ruled that a fly ball hit by the Royals' Billy Butler hit a second wall in Kansas City but was ruled a home run, which eventually proved to be the difference in a one-run Yankees loss to Kansas City.

It turns out the umpire did not know the proper ground rules.

"I figured he knew the rules," Girardi told reporters of the call, saying that in retrospect he wished he had filed a protest. "When two separate umpires with different accounts tell you, 'No, that's a home run,' I believe them. Maybe I don't need to be so trustworthy next time."

Joe learned a lesson. Next time expect him to be a little more proactive in such a situation. Joe Torre, then Major League Baseball's executive VP for baseball operations, said the umpires made the wrong call.

Also, remember Girardi's time as manager with the Marlins and his problems with ownership. Marlins owner Jeffrey Loria was getting into it with an umpire one day when Girardi essentially told Loria that enough was enough. Afterward, Girardi explained, "The gist of the conversation to Jeffrey was, 'I preach to my players about not arguing with umpires, and this is not going to help us.'"

Girardi respects authority figures. No one understands that better than Dave Rodgers, his old coach with the Sea Merchants.

"That's just the Joe I know," Rodgers said. "He put faith in his elders and was always a good listener. I think he now has become a good listener with players. In fact, I'd say he probably takes too many of other people's problems on with players, but that is just the way he is."

That's who Girardi is as a manager. You could see that in his face in times of trouble for the Yankees. That's his nature. That's how he played and now manages the game.

Rodgers is still coaching. "This is my 45th year of coaching and I still love it," he said. "I'm old school baseball, and I like to pass that along."

Rodgers began as a Pony League coach. "They first gave me a bunch of kids that couldn't play, and we won the league because I got to practice every day. When he coached Joe with the Sea Merchants he would work his practices around Joe's paper route. If the papers were late, Joe made sure not to miss practice. He'd have somebody else deliver them for him."

When he watches the Yankees on TV, he sees a different Girardi than most Yankee fans see.

"Everybody thinks he's so pensive and all that, but my Joe Girardi is sitting there going, 'I wonder if Serena has her homework done? When am I going to be able to play catch with Dante?' Some of that is going through his head, too, because he loves his children so much.

"He's not an 'alibier,' either. There were times when the Yankees had so many injuries to deal with, but he doesn't use that. He just says, 'We'll play with who we got and do the best we can.'

"Joe always said I gave him passion for the game. Passion includes losing and winning. The losing trains you for life. You get back up the next day and go at 'em."

Girardi learned all his lessons well.

"I know in the past there has been some criticism of him with the use of the pitchers," Rodgers said, "but I can't figure anybody better you want to handle the pitchers because he handled pitchers so well throughout his catching career. He probably looks deeper when he doesn't pitch a guy. Maybe he over-coaches on that sometimes, I don't know.

"He is not going to throw anybody under the bus, just to make it look good for him, and I think his players have to appreciate that," Rodgers said. "I hope they do. He's not trying to be one of them. He's a mentor."

Rodgers said all those qualities of quiet strength were evident when Girardi was 10 years old.

"He wasn't a mama's boy, he played hard," Rodgers noted. "He would take injury after injury and keep playing.

"Joe lived and died with the Cubs. If the Cubs lost, he would come to practice after his paper route with a scowl on his face," said Rodgers.

"With the Yankees he is going to give everything he can because he knows he is protecting a heritage. That's the type of guy he is. He would protect everybody on that team, from players to upper management. He would say, 'That's my fault, my responsibility. He knows the truth and he can live with the truth. A lesser man couldn't live with it.

"He knows he is in a tough spot in New York, where people are analyzing every one of his moves, but he is a Yankee. He believes in everything they do."

Rodgers believes in Girardi. He's always believed in him.

"I wear a Yankee hat around here," said Rodgers, a lifelong Cubs fan said with a laugh. "That draws more comments. I could run around naked, and they'd ask me about my hat.

"Joe has such special qualities. But I don't know if everybody in New York is going to really see them because they think of him as the Yankees manager, but he is really a special human being. What they're looking at is just one-tenth of what he really is."

Rodgers said Girardi never played the political game, that's not his nature. "He's not a hobnobber," is the way Rodgers put it. "Family is always first, and he's got extended family, too. He always wants to know how the people in the old neighborhood are doing."

The area will always be home to Joe.

Then Rodgers broke down the essence of Joe Girardi:

"Joe does a lot of stuff for a lot of people that nobody knows anything about. I know it became big news when he helped a driver in distress after he won the World Series that year, but for anybody who knows Joe—why should that surprise you? That's Joe. He would help anyone. He is not above anyone or anything. He would do it if needed. He is just going to do the right thing. If you are the manager of the Yankees, you are supposed to have special qualities. Well, Joe has special qualities. They are not always the same special qualities. He's not a Casey Stengel. He's not a Joe Torre. But he is Joe Girardi, and it's going to make a whole new mold out there. I'm sure his players realize that. I'm sure there is a difference. He likes to make a big happy family out of it. Take their problems on himself. Joe is the type that if one sheep out of a hundred gets away, he's going to chase that one sheep forever until he finds it. That's just the way he is and he's not going to make a big deal about it.

"I asked him once about A-Rod, and he said, 'I just don't talk about that stuff.' That's him. He won't talk about their [inside] stuff with anyone. The players know. You just have to watch him and how he acts. When he was a kid, he was the same way. He was the best buddy anybody could have."

5.

A-ROD AND OTHER CHALLENGES

THERE IS A GOOD reason why Alex Rodriguez is called Lightning Rod by WFAN host Steve Somers.

A-Rod is in the middle of everything. When the Yankees won the World Series in 2009, it was Alex Rodriguez who put the team on his back to carry them to their 27th world championship. Rodriguez blasted his way through the ALDS and ALCS and then along with veterans Johnny Damon and World Series MVP Hideki Matsui, finished the job in the World Series, beating the Phillies in six games.

Rodriguez hit .455 in the three-game sweep over the Twins in the ALDS with two home runs and six RBIs in his 11 at-bats. He then pounded the Angels, batting .429 as he drove in six more runs with three home runs in his 21 at-bats as he was walked eight times in the six games, giving him an on-base percentage of .567, a slugging percentage of .952, and a 1.519 OPS.

In the World Series, A-Rod drove in another six runs, giving him 18 RBIs for the 2009 postseason. While A-Rod was putting on his show, Yankees manager Joe Girardi noted of his play, "It's been as good as I can remember. What he's been able to in the postseason has been really incredible."

Then in typical Girardi fashion, he pointed to the little things because, with Girardi, it has always been the little things that make the difference.

The night before, A-Rod had had three hits, a home run, and scored three runs in a win over the Angels in Game 4 of the ALCS. Girardi pointed to the first run Rodriguez scored, breaking from third to score the first run of the game that the Yankees would go on to win 10–1.

"It's not just the home runs," Girardi said. "It's not just the RBIs. You look at the base running, him scoring on that play. The infield's in. He gets a great jump. We give our players the ability to read plays. Alex is a great base runner. His defense has been exceptional. I think his leadership has been exceptional. It's more than just the numbers sometimes, what Alex does. He's been as good as anyone I can remember."

A-Rod was certainly as good as he has ever been that October.

In all his other previous postseasons, a span of 35 games and 170 plate appearances dating back to 1995, Rodriguez had managed only 17 RBIs, yet in that single postseason, he drove in 18 runs.

That was his first postseason with Joe Girardi as his manager.

Alex Rodriguez was the lost postseason sheep, and Girardi had brought him home. When Dave Rodgers mentioned how Girardi just doesn't "talk about that stuff," Girardi's old coach knew exactly what he was talking about. Girardi goes out of his way to protect his players. That's his nature, and it's not going to change. So, when A-Rod struggled mightily in the 2011 playoffs, hitting only .111 in the five-game series loss to the Tigers in the ALDS, with a paltry .261 on-base percentage, an embarrassingly low .111 slugging percentage, and an OPS of .372, it was not surprising that, in his post-mortem of the Yankees' offensive struggles in the series,

Girardi did not pin the 3–2 loss on Rodriguez, who struck out to end the series, the third strikeout of the game for the No. 4 hitter. He protected his slugger. He pointed to the lack of "luck" Yankees hitters had at the plate against the Tigers throughout the series.

After that Game 5 loss, when Girardi was asked specifically about Rodriguez's failures in the series, and if injuries contributed to A-Rod's poor performance, he swung the answer around to make it a team failure, noting, "No, I mean, it could have been. Players aren't going to make excuses, neither am I. The bottom line is we lost some really close games to them. We lost two one-run games and a two-run game. A hit here and a hit there, and it's a different series."

For Girardi, it's never about one player or one play. He knows that Alex Rodriguez will remain with the Yankees for a long time; he is signed through 2017, and he needs to get the most out of him.

Rodriguez appreciates Girardi's managing style, going so far as to say, "He's one of my favorite guys I've met in baseball."

Rodriguez said it's not just how Girardi treats him as a player, but it is how he treats him as a person that is most impressive. Players appreciate when a manager has their backs, but it is much more than that. It's not always about baseball, and for A-Rod, a player often in the headlines for his off-the-field baseball life, the bigger picture is deeply appreciated.

"The one thing I always say about Joe that is most impressive is that baseball is secondary, which I love that," A-Rod explained. "He is a true family guy. He doesn't ask me about my swing. The first thing he wants to know is, how is Cynthia? How are the girls? How's the family? How do you feel? It's always that. And because of that, he makes me feel like I want to go out there and go through a wall for him. I love him."

Rodriguez, a star quarterback in high school, then offered this unique perspective on how Girardi runs the show with the Yankees and how he uses his coaching staff.

"He almost runs it like a football team," A-Rod said. "Like he has an offensive coordinator, a defensive coordinator, and a special-teams coach. We have the best coaching staff in baseball, in my opinion, and he really leans on his defensive coordinator, his offensive coordinator, and works really well with them. It looks like there are certain managers who don't lean on anybody, but Joe's style is very good."

When it comes to the mechanics of hitting, Girardi leaves it in the hands of hitting coach Kevin Long, one of the best in the game.

"Joe always wants to know what is going on, but he does it in a respectful way," Rodriguez said. "He's really good at not going over the head of Kevin or Mick [Kelleher, the infield coach], which is really appreciated because then there is consistency along the way. And for the players that really helps because there is less confusion. There are managers who always go over the top, but not Joe. He'll always talk to Kevin about hitting. He is always open to suggestions."

Toward the end of the 2011 season Rodriguez, 35, was bothered by a thumb injury, and Girardi allowed Long to come up with an innovative tape job on the bat, building an O-ring for A-Rod to protect his bottom thumb during the swing. Rodriguez underwent knee surgery during the season, and that greatly impacted his year, as well. It was a season filled with injuries. Rodriguez is beginning to show his age. He played in only 99 games and hit only 16 home runs and drove in 62 runs, the worst year of his career.

In so many ways, this was a much different season for Rodriguez, and Girardi had to be careful how he used him to try to get the most he could out of his aging third baseman. But this is not just about numbers and the Girardi binder that features meticulous scouting reports.

Girardi goes out of his way to make the players' families feel a part of the team.

"I love the family day," A-Rod said. "But Joe takes it a step further. Like one of the things he'll do is come up to me and ask, 'Hey, are your daughters in town?'

"I'm like, 'Yeah, they are in town for four days.'

"He'll say, 'Great, tomorrow we have 'Girls Day' in the clubhouse.' That kind of family stuff adds a personal touch," Rodriguez added. "It just changes everything and goes a long way during the season."

Those are the little things that players really appreciate. It is that kind of family attitude that bonds a team for the long season. A baseball team is together from mid-February until the end of October, if things go right.

Things didn't go right for the Yankees in 2011. They were hit with key injuries, and the pitching staff had to be reshaped. The off-season plan was to sign free agent Cliff Lee, but that didn't work out. Lee left the Rangers and signed with the Phillies.

The starting staff had to be patched together after 18-game-winner Phil Hughes suffered arm woes early in the season. Rookie starter Ivan Nova wound up becoming the Yankees' No. 2 starter for the playoffs, and in the final game he had to leave with tightness in his pitching arm. Girardi had to duct tape the final game together to keep it close, using seven pitchers, including ace CC Sabathia in relief.

In the end, though, the Yankees came up a couple base hits short of beating the Tigers. During the regular season they won the most games in the American League with 97 victories.

First baseman Mark Teixeira echoed Rodriguez's sentiments, saying, "I've always said that I respect that Joe cares for me more as a man than he does about me as a baseball player. Because he knows how hard it is to play this game. He knows there is a lot of failure involved. It's more important that we are comfortable with him as a man. He cares about our families because if that's taken care of, it makes [our time] on the field easier. Knowing how he cares about us as men, as husbands, as fathers, that allows us to do our job on the field.

"One great thing about this organization," Teixeira added, "is that Joe doesn't have to babysit. He doesn't have to make sure that guys are getting their work done. This is the hardest working group I have ever been a part of. He doesn't have to worry about guys with ulterior motives. Our motive every year is to win a World Series. So that makes it—on the field and in the clubhouse—a great atmosphere."

Superstar or rookie, Girardi tries to make each player feel at home. Girardi keeps criticism to team-wide criticism, not individual criticism.

This is the essence of his protective philosophy and the fact that he will take the bullet for his players. He would much rather have criticism thrown at him than at his players.

This is why he takes that approach.

"I believe that this game is really hard," Girardi said. "And players know when they screwed up, and you don't need to publicly talk about it. It's already bad enough. So if you have to take a bullet, you take it because I always tell people I know what really happened. I do. But I don't want players to ever feel embarrassed. I think that's the hardest part of the game when you feel embarrassed. 'Cause you're going to be hard enough on yourself. I've messed up when I thought there was two outs when there was only one out, we've all done those things. It's going to happen."

And there are times you are going to strike out to end a playoff series as Rodriguez did against the Tigers. A few days after the final loss to the Tigers, Girardi said of the season, "We all know what the goal is here. We didn't reach our goal. That's the bottom line."

The Yankees came close to making it to the ALCS for the third straight season, which would have been a tremendous achievement. It's worth noting that the Red Sox, for all their success in winning the World Series in 2004 and 2007, have not won a playoff game since October 18, 2008.

In addition, the Red Sox have missed the postseason in two of the last three seasons. It's not easy living in the AL East. After the 2011 season, the highly respected Terry Francona and the Red Sox parted ways. Two World Series championships could not help Francona salvage the season as the Red Sox collapsed down the stretch.

Nothing is guaranteed in baseball. A big payroll does not guarantee postseason success.

Deep down Girardi knows how close the Yankees came to advancing after a terrific regular season. "You look back on the [ALDS] and you lost two one-run games and a two-run game," he said. "We were a hit and maybe a couple sac flies away from still playing."

It didn't happen.

He is proud of the 2011 Yankees. Just before the playoffs began, Girardi, in a reflective moment, allowed, "This team has accomplished a lot for what we've been through."

They didn't make it to the World Series, though. They couldn't get past the Tigers, who couldn't get past the Rangers in the ALCS. The playoffs are a beast, and making it through three rounds has never been more difficult.

And when it was over, Girardi was devastated by the loss to the Tigers, saying, "Our guys played hard. I can't ask for any more from them during the course of the season. And obviously this is a terrible day for us. But we got beat."

It happens, and that is something Girardi learned growing up, something he was taught by his coaches and his parents throughout his life.

"Our pitchers threw as well as they could have this year," he added. "I really believe that. Going into spring training, with all the question marks, they pitched their hearts out. Those guys have nothing to be ashamed of. There's nothing you can really say that's going to make them feel any better. But they played their hearts out all year long."

To be knocked out so quickly, he said, was "terrible. It's a really empty feeling. It's an empty feeling for everyone in that [clubhouse]. And it hurts. You just got to remember this feeling, and we'll be determined next year."

The Yankees were "determined" to repeat in 2010, as well, but it didn't happen.

There have been no repeat champions since Joe Torre's Yankees won three straight titles in 1998, 1999, and 2000. There are new sets of challenges every year. Managers are under new sets of pressures, especially in the big markets.

Since 1977 and 1978, when the Yankees won back-to-back championships, only the Toronto Blue Jays in 1992 and 1993 managed to repeat as champions before Torre's Yankees did their thing. You have to go all the way back to 1975 and 1976 with Sparky Anderson's Big Red Machine to find an NL team that won back-to-back World Series.

Girardi will wear No. 28 again for the 2012 season. The challenge is on his back.

The goal will be the same, to try to win the World Series. That is the way of the world with the Yankees. There is pressure, but there is the understanding that the Yankees will do everything possible to put the best team on the field.

Living with that pressure is never easy, but Girardi understands the job that he signed up to do with the Yankees. He lived life in the small-market world of the Florida Marlins in 2006, his first managing job, and despite winning the BWAA's Manager of the Year honors, he was fired after the season.

The next year he went up to the TV booth, broadcasting Yankees games for YES. The following year he was named the Yankees' manager. His first season as manager, the Yankees missed the postseason for the first time since 1993. There was much work to be done, and Girardi was up to the task.

The Yankees won their 27th world championship in 2009, the first year of the new Yankee Stadium. The Yankees swept the Twins, beat the Angels in six games, and the Phillies in six, bringing home the world championship. The 114 total wins in 2009 were the second most ever in a season behind the 125 wins of the 1998 squad. That 2009 team became the first major league team to win 100 games and the World Series since Torre's 1998 Yankees. The triple layer of postseason series has made winning the World Series that much more difficult for the teams that have tremendous success during the season.

Girardi's contract takes him through the 2013 season.

He will have more chances to get back to the World Series. There will be new challenges. Girardi is ready. He has been destined to lead a baseball team since he first showed up on the campus of Northwestern University.

6.

LEADING THE WAY

JOE GIRARDI LOOKS like he could have come out of an Iowa corn-field to play pro ball. He nearly did.

After graduating Spalding Institute in 1982, where he was an all-state selection in baseball, Girardi had to decide whether to go to the University of Iowa or Northwestern. Like so many of his decisions, he sought out the advice of people close to him. One of those was his youth coach, Dave Rodgers.

"He could have very easily gone to the University of Iowa as a catcher," Rodgers explained, "but Iowa wouldn't waive the out-of-state tuition for him. I told him, 'Joe, don't go. If they want you, they'll waive the out-of-state tuition.' So he went to Northwestern. It had a better engineering school, anyway."

That turned out to be one of the best decisions of Girardi's life. Education is the insurance policy. Baseball is the icing on the cake, and Northwestern coach Ron Wellman was the perfect mentor for Girardi. "Ron Wellman influenced him a lot," Rodgers said.

Wellman, the dean of ACC athletics directors, is in his 21st season as AD at Wake Forest. He was the head coach at Northwestern for five years, compiling a 180–97 record at the school and sending 15 players onto pro ball. To this day, he remains close to Joe.

A bond was created at Northwestern between the coaching staff and the players. Paul Stevens has been the head coach at Northwestern for the last 24 seasons and is tops on the wins list for Northwestern. Stevens was an assistant under Wellman and arrived at Northwestern when Joe was a junior. To this day, the impact Girardi and Wellman had on him helped create the coach he has become, and he immediately realized what a special situation he entered.

"Ron is one of the smartest individuals I've ever been around," Stevens explained. "He definitely knew what he was doing when he was compiling the group of people he brought here to Northwestern at that time in his coaching career."

Going off to play college baseball is a life challenge, and Stevens understands the awesome responsibility and the blessing it is to be a college coach.

"I feel very blessed that I can have somebody turn over their 17-, 18-, and 19-year-old kids to me for the next four years, which will probably be as big of a groundbreaking experience for them because of the different things that they'll experience because they are getting away from home," Stevens said. "I feel fortunate to have people do that for as long as they have here at Northwestern. You know what, when you run into people like Joe and a group of other ones like Joe and you can have the worst day in the world and you think back to how blessed you are to be around people like this."

Landing Girardi was the key for Wellman. This is how he wound up with his star catcher.

"It didn't take a genius to recognize that he was very good, especially defensively," Wellman said. "After watching him one game in the state tournament, I was waiting for him after the game to talk with him, and there were seven other college coaches waiting to talk to him."

Wellman was No. 7. Girardi was doing his homework with each school.

"It took about an hour and a half to get to me," Wellman recalled. "I asked him two questions. 'What's your SAT? What's your class rank?'"

"He told me both of those, and I said, 'Would you be interested in Northwestern?'"

"By all means," said Girardi, who soon came up for a campus visit and committed to Northwestern.

"The most obvious quality he had at that point was that he was an outstanding defensive catcher," Wellman explained. "He was a good hitter, too. You could see that he had the intangibles. He loved the game. He was a great leader. He was hustling all the time. He was the heart and soul of his high school team. We were building the program at Northwestern, and we needed someone like that. He came in his freshman year and provided all those characteristics and qualities, as well."

Wellman was incredibly organized as a coach and in many ways turned the keys of his baseball kingdom over to his catcher. By the time of his senior season at Northwestern, Girardi was much more than a leader on the field and off. He was practically an assistant coach.

The team was going to fly down to the southern trip to North Carolina. Wellman, Girardi, and Grady Hall, Girardi's closest friend on the team, drove the equipment van to North Carolina. Hall ended up being a first-round draft choice of the White Sox, while Joe became a fifth-round pick of the Cubs in 1986.

"We went to Ohio the first night because my parents lived in Ohio and we stayed with them," Wellman, who was 36 at the time, said of the trip. "The next day we drove 15 hours to get to North Carolina, and it was one of the best times I have ever had. We would stop and walk in creeks and jump across creeks, and it was just time with two guys that I admired and really loved an awful lot, even though they were my players. It was just three guys who were having a ball on a road trip. I was sorry when we got there. I wanted to continue driving and having fun with them."

With a hearty laugh, Wellman added, "I felt like the younger brother a couple times because they kind of took control. I still have pictures of that trip, and every once in a while I look at them, and it always bring a smile to my face."

The future manager of the Yankees was making like Huck Finn on the trip, just enjoying the camaraderie of his friends and enjoying the country. Taking time to stop and smell the roses is a constant with Girardi. He is forever preaching to his players that he wants them to enjoy the moment, to step back from the pressure of the situation and take it all in because it is all part of the experience.

That is a side of Girardi that people in New York just can't imagine. "Believe me, he's a fun-loving guy," Wellman said.

Girardi still remembers the trip as if it were yesterday. "We had the time of our lives," Joe said. "We got out and stopped along streams. Grady was a huge baseball fan, such a Cincinnati Reds fan. And all we did was talk baseball the whole way."

Girardi remains close to his Northwestern teammates to this day. Noted Wellman, "Every once in a while we have a reunion with the Northwestern baseball players, and he is in the midst of it all. It's really interesting when they get together. They all assume the personalities and the roles that they had when they were players, and Joe falls right in. He was always a leader, always someone who was stable. He never went too far off the deep end with anything, so he was a stabilizing force."

On the field, Girardi led the way. "With Joe we had great success," Wellman said. "Two or three of the years we won over 40 games and set the number of wins for the season. We won 44 one year and went to the finals of the Big 10 championship against a Michigan team that the entire infield played major league baseball, Chris Sabo and Barry Larkin and that crew.

"Much of our success was attributable to Joe," Wellman said. "Not only because he was a great player. He was just a leader. His freshman year, he became the leader of the team and just put the team on his back."

Stevens first got to see Girardi in summer league action while he was still playing, so he saw him from that perspective as well as being a coach. "I got to know Joe totally away from Ron in that situation, and his intelligence stood out," Stevens said.

"When you first laid eyes on him, you saw a physical specimen. Joe stood out as someone you knew was going to go places. Just the charisma he had with his teammates. They bought into him. They believed in him. He wasn't somebody who was a yeller, a screamer, an intimidator. He found a way to cultivate your confidence."

Cultivating confidence is the same thing Girardi is trying to do to this day with the Yankees.

By taking the approach that he did at Northwestern, teammates were drawn to Girardi as a leader, thinking, "This guy has a lot going for him, he must know something I don't," Stevens noted. "I think that resonated all through his career the way big-time pitchers loved to throw to him and believed in him and wanted him back there because of the approach he took, the intellect. Just different things on how he studied the game. He knew situations. He'd been there, done it, and had a feeling for things. That was the part that was so evident to me."

He always had his pitcher's best interests in mind. Girardi's genius comes in a quiet way, Stevens said.

"It isn't a flaunting thing. Joe's intelligence comes out not from spewing off equations from his engineering classes, but in how perceptive he is, how he goes about his preparation and the five P's—Proper Preparation Prevents Poor Performance. Joe has always been somebody who is very, very prepared. He understands hitters. He understands the game. He understands his personnel. He understands his own strengths and weaknesses and doesn't sit there and have delusional aspects of what he can or cannot accomplish. He just finds a way to do the things that he believes in and he always has."

Girardi will do all this in his own fashion and will try to protect those around him.

"The people in New York just don't understand him taking a bullet for the people around him," Stevens said. "But that's been Joe Girardi forever, whether he realized he was taking bullets because the media was coming at somebody or he was there for his friends.

"Joe is a phenomenal individual on the field and off," Stevens said. "You don't ever want to put people on too high a pedestal, but all I can tell you is that this young man definitely has his feet firmly entrenched on the ground and he knows what he's about, and that is the part of him I absolutely love. I can't even tell you how happy I am to have had a brief opportunity to be part of his development."

The catching position is different than any other position on the field. Stevens, a former middle infielder, who was drafted by the Royals and was a member of the Topps All–Minor League Team in 1979, knows that.

"Sometimes I don't like to admit it, but they are kind of like a really good wife," Stevens said of catchers. "They are the backbone of the individual. That body of work was definitely a replication of what Joe brought to the table."

One of Girardi's great strengths is his just being there for his teammates and now for his team, as Stevens explained. "When things weren't going well, he understood you put your arm around your buddy, and when you get on him is when things are going well. Joe was always there for his teammates, when things weren't going well, letting them know that they did have the ability. They did have the capacity to work through any situation no matter what any of us coaches may or may not have been doing at that point. He always had his arm around them. That's the thing that hasn't changed, that has just stood out.

"You look at him now, how he handles people on shots in the dugout, and I can still remember that same attitude, that same approach that, 'Hey, we're behind you. You can do this. We believe in you.' That's been a constant in everything I've seen about him. He just lets people know he has faith in them. He believes in them. People react to that far better than someone jumping into their shorts and screaming up a storm. He figured that out a long, long time ago, that you are much more apt to play well if you are somewhat relaxed and have somebody say that they believe in you—if they trust what you're telling them. And I think that's another part of Joe. He gets you to trust him.

"That's how you find the intestinal fortitude to get it done, and that's the part of Joe that has always impressed me as much as anything."

This is a trait that successful coaches have always recognized about Girardi. And it doesn't take long to see this.

Dave Barnett has coached at Flagler College in St. Augustine, Florida, for 25 years. He was a graduate assistant at Iowa (1984 to 1986) when Girardi played for Northwestern. All it took was one weekend series against Northwestern to see the impact that Girardi had on his team.

"I was in charge of doing the hitting charts, and we were playing at Northwestern," recalled Barnett, who has won more than 700 games in his college coaching career. "He was a tough out, a gritty guy who just got it done. He was the biggest threat in their lineup because he was hard to strike out. He was a tough player. I was 25 years old, and I didn't look at him in awe like he is going to be a major league catcher, but he was their money guy. He was the guy you didn't want up to bat if there was a guy in scoring position in close games. I don't remember any of the other players, but I remember what a money guy Joe Girardi was for them.

"You could bet on him getting a big hit."

Like that money triple against the Braves' Greg Maddux in the Yankees' clinching Game 6 of the 1996 World Series, a victory that started a new Yankees dynasty under Joe Torre.

7.

ANGIE AND JERRY

JOE GREW UP in East Peoria, Illinois. This was the all-American family. Joe, his three brothers, and sister were never afraid of hard work. They learned that most precious gift from their parents, Angie and Jerry. Gerald Girardi worked many different jobs to provide for his family. He was a salesman, a bricklayer, a bartender, and ran his own restaurant—Girardi's.

Joe's mother was up every day at 5:00 AM, doing the laundry and getting the lunches made before she would set off for work as a child psychologist. She also worked in the restaurant as a hostess. There were mouths to feed, and education came at a price, but in the long run all those sacrifices would make the family a success.

"That work ethic was bred in me," Joe explained. "It's all I ever knew."

Work with passion. Enjoy what you do and make the most of it. Work is a major part of his life, and that is the same approach he took to the ballfield—work to get better. Keep moving forward. If something goes wrong, fix it. If a mistake is made, it is only a temporary setback. Learn from it and move forward. That's how he learned to live his life. That is how all the Girardi kids approached life.

Joe's first job was an American classic: the paper route. He worked with his dad on weekends, too, hauling bricks and at the restaurant, like all the kids did in the family, doing all the odd jobs that needed to be done to keep the restaurant going—cleaning tables, mopping floors, washing dishes, making sure the customers felt at home.

"It was a family restaurant," Joe said with a smile. "We had steak, chicken. My dad made homemade ravioli, his own sauce. It was really good."

For Joe Girardi, it is always about family and hard work, and that's exactly what he brings to the table as a manager. The jobs have changed through the years, but the approach is the same— work hard and work with a purpose, arrive early and stay late, do what has to be done, and better yet, if you can do it as a family, it is all that much more rewarding.

One of Joe's proudest moments was when he bought that first car, a rite of passage for any teenager. "A Ford Tempo," Girardi said with a smile. "That was a great car."

Joe also got creative, too, when it came to raising extra money to buy that car.

"We had a German shepherd," he said. "She had puppies, and I sold the puppies."

Maybe there is a little GM in Girardi as well as being a manager.

When his dad worked as a salesman, Joe would go on trips with him, as would the other children, John, George, Jerry, and Maria.

"We used to listen to Cubs games," Joe said of those wonderful summer days. "He would take me, and I would go into the sales calls with him. He was a true blue Cubs fan, and he brainwashed all his kids."

Imagine those drives, father and son moving through the heart of the country, listening to Cubs games. That is how Joe's passion for the Cubs came to being. That is how Joe Girardi became a Cubs fan, a team he would be drafted by and play his first four major league seasons with and return to eight years later to play three more years toward the end of his playing career.

In so many ways, the Cubs were home.

There were other trips, too. Fishing was always a big event for the Girardi family.

"I used to love to go fishing with my dad," Joe said.

Jerry Girardi had a way to make all the kids feel like "real" fishermen when they would go after the big catfish that Jerry loved to catch.

"We used to fish for bullheads, and my dad would have two hooks on each pole—he would catch them and let us reel them in," Joe recalled, the memory bringing a huge smile to his face.

"I thought I was reeling in a shark. I'm six, seven years old, and it was just so much fun. I remember one time we had three poles going and another one on the dock. A couple bullheads hit and took one of the poles into the water. My brother George had to go in and get it. We just loved to go fishing with my dad."

There were plenty of family antics along the way.

"We went on a Canadian fishing trip, and I tipped the boat over on my dad accidentally when he told me to pull it to the side," Joe said. "He got mad at me because his tackle box was open. I was only eight or nine years old. I guess I leaned on the boat when I pulled it in."

There also was the time when Joe was very young and decided he needed to help his dad "clean" the fish. Joe and a friend, who were both about seven at the time, rounded up every household cleaner they could find and put the cleaning agents into the bucket of bullheads that Jerry had caught early in the morning. Jerry then went to work. He was going to clean the fish when he got home from work. There was going to be a feast of catfish for dinner.

The fish were clean, that's for sure, clean dead. When Jerry came home, he was quite upset, but realized Joe and his friend were just trying to help. There would be no fried catfish that night for dinner, but Joe had a lifetime story to tell about how he first learned to "clean" fish.

Joe and his dad often would play basketball. They would wrestle, too. Those are two ways Joe learned about physical toughness. His father would not take it easy on him in those games of one-on-one. It was a physical as well as a mental battle, and it all helped shaped Joe's ability to weather any athletic storm. It was all part of growing up in the Girardi household, and raising a family is a 24/7 job, the best job anyone could have.

Joe loved every moment. Lessons were learned.

"The wrestling with my dad, and him pinning us down, him rubbing his beard on us, it was all that," Joe said. "Teaching us to love the game, teaching us toughness. It was all that."

Most of all, though, it was about time, just spending time with his parents.

"I remember the time that my father and mother always gave to us, and I loved it," Joe said. "And I just love being a husband and a father. It's really the center of my life."

The Girardi family did things as a family, and that left a lasting imprint on Joe and guides him to this day with his family life. "That's why Kim and I love to spend time with our children," he said. "My mom and dad did the same thing. It was all I knew."

That's the joy of being a parent—spending time with your children as they grow up and watching them grow and mature in so many ways. Those kinds of experiences are priceless.

All the lessons paid off, as Joe went on to star in high school in baseball and football, a catcher and a quarterback, a leader all the way in each sport, a teammate you could lean on.

Dave Rodgers, the Sea Merchants coach, said, "Jerry worked hard, and the family never wanted for anything. And Joe's mother was a saint. She made sure all the boys and girls had a good education. They played hard. They did everything with enthusiasm, and she followed them with everything they did."

When the toughest times came, as they did when Joe's mom was diagnosed with terminal cancer, they stuck together as a family, too.

"She was very small in stature, maybe 5'1", and maybe 110 pounds, but her heart was incredibly big and she was tough," Joe said of his mom. "She persevered as much as anyone I've ever seen. When she was diagnosed, she was given three months, and she wasn't ready to go."

No she wasn't. There was still a family to help raise, and seeing all her kids get an education was the No. 1 goal for Angie.

That and baseball helped keep her alive for another six years. She wanted to see Joe achieve success in the game. She wanted to see all her children get an education. She was there for them. She saw two of her sons get into medical school; saw Joe get into Northwestern, where he was a three-time academic All-American; watched her daughter graduate college; and was there as her youngest graduated high school.

"As kids, we all felt we gave her something to live for in what we were doing," is the way Joe put it, the inner goal of making the most of yourself through education. "And probably about the third year, she missed my sister's high school graduation because she was too sick to go. I think she was at the Mayo Clinic. She said before she passed, she wanted to see my sister graduate and her two sons get into med school. Well, it all happened in early June, and she passed away about two weeks later in the sixth year, and that was it. My sister actually graduated college in three years."

Three years. The clock was ticking, and family dreams needed to be fulfilled, no matter the obstacle. Joe found his success in the world of baseball, two brothers became doctors, his youngest brother is an accountant, and Maria is a distinguished math professor at the University of South Carolina. That hard work paid off in so many ways and continues to pay off in so many ways every day.

Even though she was battling a deadly disease every day, Angie focused on a brighter future for her children, and that is how she managed to carry on through those most difficult and painful times. It really all came down to one word: hope.

"My mom had hope," Joe explained. "She had a tremendous relationship with God, and I think she knew what she wanted in life. And she wanted to make sure that all her kids were okay. I was out in the Cape [Cod League] playing, and my youngest brother would have been a senior in high school, just finishing his senior year in high school when she died. It was probably toughest on him, Jerry, because he was the youngest. But it was really difficult on all our family."

They stayed together as a family for the entire time his mom was sick.

"My dad was a rock through all of it," Joe said.

"So was my mom. I remember days when she said, 'Make sure I don't take too much medicine,' because she would get so sick from the chemo. She'd have a little bit of yogurt that her friends made for her that she would eat.

"My mother continued to work through all of it," Joe added. "She never stopped working as a child psychologist. She worked for the district. She'd get up and make our lunches every morning and do the laundry, and my father was right there."

Joe said he remembers his mom's final words to him: "Don't forget me."

He never will, of course, and every day he remembers her by honoring her with his work ethic and with his duties as a father and husband.

Angie and Jerry also left a tremendous impression on all of Joe's coaches through the years.

"I'm very grateful that I've had a lot of opportunities to be around Joe and his father," said Northwestern coach Paul Stevens. "His father was one of the true blue-collar human beings, a guy who was willing to roll up his sleeves and do anything he had to do for his family and others. I can't even tell you what a great man he was. I just wish I would have gotten to know him when he was 20 or 30 just to see if he was a lot like his son. The Girardi family is something special."

Joe's mom and dad proved to be perfect role models, and Joe and Kim strive to be the same kind of role models for Serena, Dante, and Lena.

"We met in college," Joe said of Kim. "We knew each other for a couple of years, she was a year behind me, and we went out on a date, and I told my friend, 'That's the girl I'm going to marry.' Her roommate and my former roommate were dating, and we went, for whatever reason, to an Olympic wrestling match at Northwestern and then to a frat party afterward.

"We are complete opposites," Joe added with a smile. "She's the risk-taker. I'm the conservative one. She's the spice of our life."

"Make no mistake about Kim," Stevens noted. "She means so much to Joe. Those two are involved in so many different things that mean so much to so many different people in a quiet way. I know what Joe has done for this program behind the scenes even when he wasn't in the big leagues and making a lot of money. Kim and Joe are involved in so much. It's in places where they don't care if they get any recognition. It's about what they feel they've been blessed with and how they can help and bless somebody else.

I think their faith and their spirit of generosity and compassion, it all boils down to character and values. It's pretty amazing in today's day and age."

For Joe, it all goes back to how he was raised by Angie and Jerry. Doing the job right matters greatly no matter how big or small the task. Staying together as a family will get you through the tough times. You win together as a team. When his teams lose, Girardi takes it hard, but he also understands that baseball allows you to come back the next day or the next season.

Baseball is a game filled with tomorrows. There is always tomorrow in baseball. There is always hope. For Joe, baseball became much more than a game.

Joe used to think that playing baseball was his way of helping keep his mom alive. It wasn't until Kim told him that he had a gift and that baseball would be a platform of future success for him that he truly understood where his place in the game would be and that he could become a major league player. He had the talent, he had the desire, and he was pushed to succeed by himself and his family.

"We were forced to grow up early because of what we were going through in our household," Joe said. "And I had older brothers who always pushed me athletically, and I think that helped me because I always played ahead. When I was 10, I was playing with kids who were 11 and 12. When I was 14, I was playing with kids who were 16- and 17-year-olds. It all just kind of made me grow up a little bit faster."

"I know it's tough on Joe with his dad," Dave Rodgers said. "It's an emotional moment for Joe. He's playing in the playoffs, and I know he's sitting there thinking about his dad sitting in a wheelchair in a nursing home."

Patience and a prayerful life were learned at home.

"Joe doesn't rush into anything," said his former college coach Ron Wellman. "He makes a logical, prayerful decision. He's a believer. He's committed his life to Christ. He doesn't necessarily wear it on his sleeve, but he lives that life. He honors his values. He follows his values. I've talked to him a number of times about decisions he is making in his life, and what he always says is that, 'I've prayed about this and I believe God is leading me in this direction.' That's a beacon in his life, and he doesn't do anything without prayerful consideration."

"His mom and dad were very committed Christians," Wellman said. "His mother was one of the toughest and nicest people I've ever met. She was just a wonderful lady. When we met her, she had terminal cancer, and she lived three more years after that in pain, yet you would never know it. She was one of the most positive, upbeat, wonderful people I've ever known."

It was the summer after Joe's junior season at Northwestern when his mother passed away. Even in those final, most difficult days, she remained strong. Inner strength survives no matter the burden. Listen to this story from Ron Wellman. "We had gone down to visit her that summer in the hospital, and she was sleeping," Wellman recalled. "My wife and I just stood there for an hour as she slept, and we decided to write her a note and take off. When we were leaving, though, she woke up and scolded us, saying, 'How could you leave without waking me up and talking with me?'

"Joe was so very close to her," Wellman said, "and she held him accountable. There was a love between them that is hard to describe because he was just like her. He had all of her qualities and characteristics. You could tell whenever they were together there was a tremendous feeling of love for one another."

Joe was a dutiful son and listened to his mother. "His mother wanted him to have a Catholic education, that's why he went to Spalding," Dave Rodgers said.

Wellman said that Jerry Girardi was always a man of solid character.

"He had tremendous pride in his children," Wellman said. "Every time you saw him, he was gracious, he was kind, but he didn't have to be front and center with everything. He just kind of fit into the crowd and just really enjoyed everyone, and everyone had tremendous respect and appreciation for him.

"I never had a problem with his parents."

For a coach, that is the best situation possible, a gifted player to lean on, a leader, and parents who were extremely supportive in everything that the coach did for the program.

"You can rely upon them," Wellman said. "You never have to be concerned what they are doing and what they are saying behind your back. They are never concerned about the role of their son. They just accept the coach's decisions."

Wellman then laughed and added, "Of course, all my decisions were for Joe."

Of course they were. Joe was the rock of the program. That's good coaching, making the most of his players' talents and realizing Joe was a leader, and that is exactly what Wellman did with Girardi. For a baseball team to be successful, there has to be leadership from within, it has to start with the players, and the players have to have internal leadership, it cannot all fall on the coach. The same goes for any level—high school, college, or the major leagues.

All of Joe's coaches recognized the same great leadership traits in Girardi. The special ones always stand out, and even more so in a game and in a society where accountability is not as valued or as prominent as it once was. Just look at the daily headlines in sports and in other areas.

"Joe is accountable because he cares about the people he works for," Stevens said. "That drives him. He is accountable for winning, and it does affect him, and that's because he's accountable for what goes on, and he takes that very seriously.

"He is a man who puts God very high on his priority list," Stevens said. "I know that God is one and family is two with him. Joe has definitely taken his hands off the wheel and said, 'You know what, steer me where you need me to go.'"

Follow the guiding light, and you find success as a player and as a person. No matter what, Joe knows there is always hope.

8.

THE WISDOM OF ZIM

JOHN STERLING IS blessed with a booming voice and a booming personality. He is at every Yankees game. He is a constant with the fans and the team. His voice is one of the most recognized voices in the game. Over the last 23 seasons, Sterling has broadcast nearly 4,000 Yankees games, and each day he offers up the pregame manager's report, spending time with Joe Girardi.

"There is nothing that isn't decent about Joe Girardi," Sterling began, his voice in full Broadway mode, setting the stage for the following story that best relates how he feels about Girardi.

"In a hotel in Fort Worth—The Worthington—several years ago," Sterling began in his wonderful "the Yankees win" style, "I just happen to get on the elevator, and Don Zimmer and Joe Girardi are on the elevator.

"Well, Girardi is on a lower floor; he gets off, and Zimmer turns to me and says, 'John, in my 50 years in baseball, he is the single, nicest human being I've ever met.'

"That says it all."

It sure does. Donald William Zimmer is a baseball icon. He has met everyone in the game over the course of his amazing career, which began in 1949 with the Cambridge Dodgers in Cambridge, Maryland, in the Eastern Shore League. The next season, Zimmer played in Hornell, New York, in the Pennsylvania-Ontario New York League. His life in baseball is an A to Z experience, all you have to do is look at the rosters Zimmer has been on through the years. In fact, in those first two years alone, it was an A to Z experience—Andrew Alexson to Zeke Zeisz.

Zimmer's journey is really the ultimate baseball journey.

Look at his picture on the terrific website Baseball-reference.com and you see a young Zimmer full of anticipation of what will come next in his baseball life. Zimmer embraced the game, and the game has never let him down. The road has been long. The infielder was a Brooklyn Dodger and made the move west to Los Angeles. He played for the Cubs and later managed the Cubs. He was an original New York Met, acquired in the premium phase of the 1961 expansion draft. He finished his playing career in Washington with the Senators. He started and finished with two franchises that moved on, just like he has moved on over his 63 years in the game.

He has played, coached, and managed, and is now a senior advisor for the Tampa Bay Rays. "Zim will remain with the Rays as long as he wants," explained principal owner Stuart Sternberg. "We all love Zim. He is a baseball institution."

The game and the people remain close to Zim's heart.

Through the years, Zimmer has been teammates with, coached, or managed seemingly everyone in post–World War II baseball. The list is a Who's Who. In Brooklyn there was Jackie Robinson, Pee Wee Reese, Gil Hodges, Roy Campanella, Johnny Podres, Duke Snider, Don Newcombe, Sal Maglie, and a couple of young lefty pitchers. One went to the Hall of Fame as a pitcher, Sandy Koufax, who won three world championships, posting a World Series ERA of 0.95 over eight October games. In 1963 Koufax' 2–0 performance in two starts against the Yankees (23 strikeouts in 18 innings) prompted Yogi Berra, another baseball icon, to say,

"I can see how he won 25 games. What I don't understand is how he lost five."

The other lefty went to the Hall of Fame as a manager, Tommy Lasorda, leading the Dodgers to eight division titles and two world championships in 21 seasons as a manager.

Zimmer was a member of the 1955 Brooklyn team that beat the Yankees in the World Series in seven amazing games. His roommate, back when major league players had roommates, was Johnny Podres, who won Games 3 and 7 to earn MVP honors. Game 7 was a 2–0 victory at Yankee Stadium in front of 62,465 fans. In the sixth inning of that Game 7, Walter Alston pinch-hit for Zimmer, his second baseman. Alston moved left-fielder Jim Gilliam to second and inserted Sandy Amoros into left. Amoros then made one of the greatest catches of all-time—the greatest World Series Game 7 catch ever—with the potential tying runs on base, he snared Yogi Berra's slicing fly ball in the left-field corner and then doubled Gil McDougald off first base.

Berra hit .417 in the World Series. He should have hit .458. Zimmer often jokes that he helped win the World Series by being taken out of that game.

Zimmer played 12 years in the majors with five different teams. He managed 13 years in the majors, beginning with the San Diego Padres in 1972. In 1976 he moved to the Red Sox, where he managed Carl Yastrzemski and Carlton Fisk and tried to manage "the Spaceman," Bill Lee. He went on to manage the Texas Rangers and Cubs. He has either played, coached, or managed in pro ball since 1949, and of all the people he has met in the game, he lists Girardi as "the single nicest human being."

In 1989 Zimmer won the Manager of the Year award with the Cubs. The club won 93 games and finished first in the NL East. Girardi, 24, was a rookie on that team. They lost in the NLCS to the Giants in five games. In their only victory, Girardi was the starting catcher for Zimmer in a 9–5 Game 2 win. Girardi played in four of the playoff games.

A lifelong friendship was formed. "I love Zim," Girardi said. It was Zimmer, who as a coach for Joe Torre with the Yankees, always stood up for Girardi in organizational meetings with George Steinbrenner and the Yankees brass. Zimmer knew that in so many ways Girardi was the glue that held the pitching staff together during Girardi's playing years in New York.

Girardi played 379 games with the Yankees from 1996 to 1999 and another 35 games in the postseason. He batted .272, but he was much more important than numbers could show. He tutored Jorge Posada on the art of catching and was there for the pitching staff in every way as the Yankees won three world championships during those four seasons, an incredible run.

With the Cubs, Zimmer loved the way Girardi approached the game and everything else about the young catcher. Here's what first caught Zimmer's eye about Girardi.

"He was an outstanding catcher, knew how to play the game, always did the right things on the field," Zimmer said. "I always put it this way: Joe Girardi could be anything he wanted to be. If he wanted to be an engineer, he could be an engineer, that's what he went to school to study. If he wanted to be a coach, he'd be a coach. If he wanted to manage, he'd be a manager. That's the way I always felt about him because he is just a solid person who had baseball knowledge for sure."

Those words should not be taken lightly for Zimmer.

"He's the all-American boy," Zimmer said.

Girardi wasn't perfect. "He was not a great hitter, but he was a good hitter," Zimmer noted. "He was the best bunter I had on the club. He could steal a base when you wanted it stolen."

Reflecting on Girardi's career from the first time he saw him in Cubs camp to now, manager of the Yankees with a World Series championship under his belt, an NL Manager of the Year award (his one season with the Marlins), and the respect of his peers in the game, Zimmer said, "What he's done and where's been doesn't surprise me one bit."

Bringing an engineering background to baseball has been vital to his success. "He's very intelligent," Zimmer said.

Zimmer is one of Torre's greatest friends in the game. He has the utmost respect for Torre, who was Commissioner Bud Selig's right-hand man as executive VP of baseball operations before becoming part of a group trying to buy the Los Angeles Dodgers. Following Torre as manager of the Yankees was not an easy task for Girardi in 2008, especially with the Yankees failing to make the postseason for the first time since 1993. Still, that team won 89 and lost 73 in a year of much-needed transition.

The way Zimmer sees it, going from Torre to Girardi was the perfect transition for the Yankees. "Nobody is going to take Joe Torre's spot," said Zimmer, who is still on top of his game at the age 81. "Joe Torre is Joe Torre. Joe Girardi is Joe Girardi. Both are great people." When asked about Girardi's loyalty, Zimmer smiled and said, "Oh, my God. That's where Joe Girardi and Joe Torre come into effect, loyalty. Loyalty has kind of left our game to a certain respect, but these two guys have loyalty."

Girardi was with the Cubs the first time around, from 1989 through 1992, batting .262 during that span. His job was to take care of the pitchers, get the most out of them, and everything else was a bonus. Pitching at Wrigley Field is never easy, and Girardi had to coax his pitchers through some tough times. Mark Grace was a teammate in Chicago with Girardi. Grace was a star player at the time. He had respect for how Girardi approached the game.

"Joe was mostly a backup catcher, he had to make himself that everyday player," Grace said. "He understood he had to grind it out."

Grinding it out, day by day, that's the only way Girardi knew how to succeed. It's like hitting the gym every day. You make the most of what you have, you make yourself as strong as you can mentally and physically—those are the characteristics that defined Girardi when he first came up to the National League as he had to establish himself.

That is what really impressed Grace, not Girardi's ability, his mental and physical toughness in an everyday way. Somehow Girardi came through his career without suffering any major injuries. "I don't ever remember even getting a concussion," Girardi said. He then laughed and added, "Hard head, I guess."

Grace knew what made Girardi tick as a player.

"You could always tell how much he cared," said Grace, a first baseman, who hit .310 from 1988 to 1999. Grace was Mr. Consistency at the plate for the Cubs. "Joe would take losses hard. It was right back to the drawing board for him after a loss. You could tell how much he cared about his pitcher during the game. He cared about that as much as he cared about his own game, and that's the impressive thing for me."

For Girardi, it was all about the game and representing the Cubs in the right way. Grace, who has been known to have his fun, noted: "Joe wasn't a rabble-rouser in the clubhouse. Joe just went out there and played. He was fun in the clubhouse, don't get me wrong. But he was never a guy you could tell stories about that he was out all night getting drunk or had a lamp shade on his head."

Grace then smiled and said, "I got those stories, but Joe doesn't have those stories."

A manager has to manage all types of players. That is the hardest part of the job, and Zimmer has seen all kinds of players come through the clubhouse through the years. Girardi was a player who worked overtime to overcome his shortcomings.

"Joe did everything that was asked of him," Zimmer said. Remember, only Zimmer has this kind of wealth of firsthand baseball knowledge and personal experience to make the following statement about Girardi.

"He was not a Roy Campanella who hit 30 to 40 home runs," Zimmer said. "He was not a Yogi Berra who hit 30 home runs and drove in 100 runs. But he did little things to help you win games. He could steal a base. He would hit the ball to the right side. He was a good hit-and-run man. He was just a complete player, but never had the qualities to be a star. He was a good solid player."

Girardi is a solid person all the way. Anyone who really knows him always wants to talk about his wife, Kim, how strong a presence she is in his life and about Girardi's characteristics as a father and husband. Zimmer is no different.

"Joe is a tremendous family man, and Kim is a special girl," Zimmer said. "Joe has a wonderful wife and children, I can't say enough about him. That's all there is to it. They are special people."

Girardi's eyes light up whenever he sees Zimmer. The same goes for Zimmer.

"The closeness that we had," Zimmer explained, "is always there. You see, the first 10 years he spent in the big leagues, I spent with him. I was with him in Chicago when he was a rookie playing for me. I went to Colorado as a coach. He followed me. I went to New York. He followed me. Everybody thought I had something to do with it all the time, but really I had nothing to do with it. It kind of just worked that way."

Sometimes, that's just the way baseball works.

Zimmer then pointed out a game experience that put Girardi's career in perspective, and again, remember, this from someone who has been involved in roughly 11,000 games over the course of his career and has been a manager or coach in three baseball cathedrals, Wrigley Field, Fenway Park, and Yankee Stadium. Zimmer did not choose a game where Girardi got a big hit or made a great defensive play.

Zimmer chose an incident where Girardi messed up as a way to show Girardi's accountability.

"We would always talk about Wrigley Field being an easy park to hit a home run in, especially when the wind was blowing out," Zimmer said. "In a one-run game, you never want a home run hitter to hit anything from the middle in. You want to be low and outside. If he hits it out in right field, all right, you tip your hat. We were playing this game, and I see Joe setting up outside corner, outside corner, outside corner, and then all of a sudden he shifted inside, and the guy hit a home run."

Zimmer filed the information away. He was upset.

"The next day I said to him, 'Joe, what the hell is going on?' In a one-run situation late in the game, you stay away from the hitter.'

"He had a reason, and I said, 'That reason is no good.' I was hot," Zimmer recalled.

"I went home and thought about it and said to myself, 'Here's my, not exactly my best player, but a guy I depended on,' and I felt really bad. The next day I called him in and said, 'I'm sorry I got on your ass.'

"You know what he said?

"He said, 'You should have.'"

Accountability is important to Girardi, and there was evidence of a young player standing up and taking the heat. A lot of players would have taken Zimmer's harsh words personally; Girardi took it as a learning experience and owned up to it. Mistakes are made in this game. Baseball is a relentless challenge, physically and mentally, a grind. Girardi made a big mistake that day, but he learned from it and told his manager that he was at fault even though his manager was looking to give the young catcher a pass.

In the journey of 63 years in baseball, this is just one small story, one of thousands of stories that Zimmer has about the game, but for Zimmer it told the story of what kind of player, what kind of person Joe Girardi was then and is today as manager of the Yankees.

There's one other story Zimmer wanted to relate about Girardi the young catcher.

"He and my second-string catcher were wearing thumb guards," Zimmer explained. "So with a man on third base, the ball bounces off Joe and goes to the screen. I go to him, 'The next time I see that thumb guard…!' I don't know what I said, but it wasn't good. I said I don't want to see any more thumb guards.'

"He said, 'Okay, okay.'

"He got rid of the thumb guard. He always took advice, even harsh advice the right way," Zimmer said. "He understood that I was trying to make him a better ballplayer."

Girardi always called his own game with Zimmer as the manager. "I never called pitches for him," Zimmer explained. "He called the game. I would never question him during a game. After the game I might say, 'In that situation, why did you call a curveball?' He gave me his answer; that was good enough for me. I knew what he was doing. It wasn't that he was just putting down fingers; he had an idea what he was doing. He had a plan."

"He did the little things he had to do to be a good player. He knew his capabilities. Above everything else, Joe Girardi is a winner."

9.

ONE JOE TO ANOTHER

AS A PLAYER, Joe Girardi was blessed to have Don Zimmer as his first major league manager with the Cubs in 1989. When the catcher was taken by the Rockies in the 1992 expansion draft, Don Baylor, another tremendous individual, became his manager. After the 1995 season, Girardi was traded to the Yankees. Another catcher, Joe Torre, was at the helm, and he even helped navigate the trade that brought Girardi to New York.

Girardi had the opportunity to learn from the best along the way.

"Joe is very bright and very aware," Torre began. "And he has a feel. [As] a catcher—especially being around Zim earlier in his career—he learned a lot of lessons about the game. Then, as a coach with the Yankees, he had the opportunity to learn the game from that perspective.

"Being Yankees manager, that was going to be Joe's job, if it was ever available. That job was the only one that he ever wanted. This is a dream job for him, and he is at a great age for it."

Torre said the way Girardi played the game set him up for his managerial career. It's as if Girardi was always putting the pieces in place to become a manager.

As a Yankees player, Girardi played a pivotal role in how Torre first managed when he took over the team in 1996. How important a role did Girardi play? Consider that Girardi played the role of Derek Jeter until Jeter was ready to accept the responsibility of being Mr. Yankee.

"Even though he was an ordinary player," Torre explained, "Joe was such an important piece for our '96 club. He did so many things for us. He batted second. He did the squeeze. He was really my sounding board. He was that player. Eventually, I went to Jeter, but it was unfair for me to go to Jeter at such a young age in 1996."

Torre was in the cauldron of New York Yankees baseball with George Steinbrenner being the one and only Boss. He needed players he could lean on; he needed Joe Girardi.

Torre recognized right away the leadership qualities of Girardi, who was 31 years old at the time and was entering his eighth season in the majors. But it was his first year in the American League, after playing four seasons with the Cubs and then three years helping to establish the Colorado Rockies franchise.

"Joey just had a feel for stuff," Torre explained. "And when he came back as a coach for me [in 2005], he knew how to use technology. He was far beyond me in that way. Donnie Mattingly was the same way with that, and they bonded in their use of technology."

Girardi has gotten the chance to experience baseball in New York City and feel the passion of the Yankees fans in three different ways—as a player, a coach, and a manager who brought home the World Series in 2009.

After years with the valiant Cubs fan base and then helping to create a new fan base in Colorado, Girardi came to a proud franchise whose fans desperately wanted their team to be on top again in 1996. "Baseball fans are very deep-seated; they are not casual," noted Torre. "It is part of their life."

Torre said Girardi first caught his eye as a player when he was with the Rockies. "I just liked the way he did the job of catching," Torre said. "As a former catcher myself, I looked for certain things, and it looked like he had the take-charge quality, which is so necessary."

There is a fine line between taking charge and acting like you are in charge. Joe Torre began his major league career with the Milwaukee Braves in 1960. This is 51 years of baseball wisdom speaking. "The take-charge quality is not necessarily to be demanding as a catcher, but it's to have the pitcher trust you," Torre explained. "Joe had that way about him, which was sort of a good balance forcing, and yet, having the pitcher understand, and that's what really caught my eye. Maybe if I didn't play that position, I wouldn't really recognize it, but I did.

"So I ran it by Zim. I asked him about Girardi before I talked to [GM] Bob Watson about making a move and trying to do this," Torre said of the trade that brought Girardi to the Yankees for right-handed pitcher Mike DeJean.

Torre added with a smile, "I thought it was a perfect move even though [Jorge] Posada didn't like me very much for making it because it sort of slowed his progression at that point."

Girardi loved every minute of playing for the Yankees and learning under Joseph Paul Torre, who 30 years earlier had hit .315 for the Braves in 1966 and had made the All-Star team for the fourth straight season. There was much to learn. By 1996 Torre already had 14 years of managing under his belt with the Mets, Braves, and Cardinals.

"I loved playing for Joe," Girardi said. "I had the chance to play for three championship teams under Joe, which was awesome. He took me under his wing in 2005 as his bench coach and was very open, allowed me to do a lot of things for which I am forever grateful."

The atmosphere that Joe Torre created with his coaches allowed Girardi to blossom.

"He was a mentor for me," Girardi said. "He was a manager I found it easy to play for. Not that I really found any managers hard to play for, but Joe had a calmness about him in a place that is not always so calm, and it made you feel like everything was going to be okay if we stuck together. And for the years that I was here, he was usually right. Three out of the four years I was fortunate enough to win a ring as a player here, so he meant a lot."

No matter how many great lessons Torre taught Girardi, there is nothing like the personal experience of being Yankees manager.

"I don't think you really know what this job is like until you sit in the manager's chair," Girardi said with a chuckle. "I was fortunate enough that Joe let me sit around him when he did a lot of his things and let me watch it. It's a lot different when you have to answer for the moves, as opposed to watching someone answer for the moves. I think you watch someone do it, you have an understanding of why he did it, but just allowing me to sit next to him when he managed games, to throw any idea out there, I am very thankful. It was his decision to decide what he wanted to do, but those are the things that you learn. You learn there is a lot you have to deal with when you sit in this chair."

Torre could relate to that comment, 100 times over. "That is the toughest thing, baseball aside," Torre admitted. Then Torre offered this peek into his managerial mindset, a similar approach that Girardi takes with him to the dugout every game.

"I'm not necessarily one who believes 'right move/wrong move,'" Torre explained. "I just believe there are moves that work and moves that don't work. That's the toughest part of the job, dealing with the media, and it's getting tougher and tougher because everybody wants instant stuff all the time."

Torre is so right about that. There has never been a more instant, judgmental media than in this day and age. In the instant land of Twitter, Facebook, blogs, columns, videos, talk radio, and talking heads on TV, every move is overanalyzed.

But that's also what makes baseball so great—it goes back to Torre's comments about baseball fans having such passion for their team and for the game. Even with all the prying eyes, the manager can never overlook the Big Picture.

"It's tough doing that with 162 games, and what may be bad today, the bad part may turn out to be a help later on because you are dealing with individuals," Torre explained. "You have to pretty much stay the course with guys you trust as players."

Sometimes you have to rest players down the stretch or nurse them through injuries when a division title may be on the line, as Girardi had to do in 2010, essentially making sure the Yankees got into the postseason in the best physical shape possible, even if it cost them the AL East.

That year the Yankees made it to the ALCS before losing to the Rangers. In 2011 they won the AL East, posted the best record in the American League, but could not get past the Tigers in the division series, losing because they could not come up with the crucial hit. There is no blueprint to the World Series. It changes year to year. In the 2011 playoffs, Alex Rodriguez batted .111. Mark Teixeira hit .167, Russell Martin batted .176, and Nick Swisher checked in with a .211 average against Detroit.

A short series is a test of wills.

Sometimes, no matter how you plan it, it doesn't work out. In that five-game series, the Yankees outscored the Tigers 28–17 but lost three of the five games, two by one run and one by two runs.

In that respect it was similar to the 1960 World Series the Yankees lost in seven games to the Pirates. Over those seven games, the

Yankees outscored the Pirates 55–27, but came up short in the seventh game. That's baseball.

Torre loved what Girardi did in 2009 with the key move of the postseason. "He took some criticism for going with the three-man rotation, and sitting 3,000 miles away, I certainly understood what he was doing and agreed with it."

Torre was on the other end of such a decision during the 2003 World Series, Marlins manager Jack McKeon went with the decision to pitch Josh Beckett in Game 6 at Yankee Stadium on short rest. Beckett pitched a complete-game shutout, winning the World Series for the Marlins with the 2–0 victory. McKeon's move paid off in a big way.

Said Torre, "Jack would have been really criticized if he had lost, 'Why did you do that? You could have had him at full rest?' But when you get in a short series, we were up 2–1, and then they had us where they were up 3–2, you don't want us to gain back traction. That's the whole thing about short series, one game is a tremendous momentum turner."

Torre knows all about momentum shifts in a series, and in that World Series against the Marlins, Florida shortstop Alex Gonzalez hit a series-changing home run in Game 4 in the 12th inning off Jeff Weaver, who had just pitched a 1-2-3 11th inning.

"You know what I really felt bad about was that Weaver was just on the way back," Torre said, looking back on that World Series, "gave up the home run, I think it was a 2–0 pitch [3–2, actually]. I'd rather him do that than walk the guy because [Gonzalez] is not really a home run hitter."

Reflecting on the results of that day, Torre added, "I'm sitting there, and I said to [Brian Cashman], 'We might as well trade him because I don't think he'll ever be able to work his way back again.' I felt so badly because he did the right thing."

Less than two months later, Weaver was traded to the Dodgers in a deal for Kevin Brown.

In the postseason, one pitch can change a career.

A manager has to grow with each season, as well, and Torre has seen that growth in Girardi. As a manager with four championship rings, Torre knows most of all, "Nobody can take a world championship away from you, and making the decisions that he had to make, what happened in '08 was probably the best way to sort of flush out everything and start '09 fresh. Joe just seems more and more confident each year."

Torre, like Girardi, understands how difficult the game can be in New York and in the American League East with all the battles with the Boston Red Sox. Yes, it is a game, but it's never really fun in the sense of pure enjoyment.

"It was never fun," Torre noted. "It was exciting. It was gratifying. You felt when you accomplished something, it was something special. There was never mediocre stuff going on. Nothing was ever okay.

"With those Red Sox series, Terry Francona and I used to talk after every series and say, 'Thank God this is over for another six weeks,' or whatever. We respected the hell out of each other, but we knew it was a war. And now that same atmosphere has been created with Tampa Bay. And Tampa was always on our radar screen because of George living down there. George in spring training was funny. He used to complain because we only beat them by two runs, in spring training games! You couldn't laugh, but you were amused because it was spring training, but that's how George was, and he felt embarrassed because they were an expansion team."

Girardi was able to get George Steinbrenner his last World Series ring.

When Torre returned to Yankee Stadium for the first time in 2010, three years after his Yankees managerial career came to an end, for the unveiling of the George Steinbrenner plaque in Monument Park, Girardi was one of the first Yankees to welcome him home to the new Yankee Stadium.

"I'm glad he's back," Girardi said that night. "Joe was a big part of the run that happened here. The success that the Yankees have had over the last 15 years, Joe was here for most of it. I think it means a lot. It was nice to see him out in L.A., but it's also nice to see him come home. This is where he was raised; it's good to see him come home. He's happy to be back. He and Donnie signed the wall in the clubhouse."

The Yankees have a wall in their clubhouse area that is off-limits to the media. It is a sacred place. "Anyone who has played for the Yankees signs it," Girardi said. "When players who are now on other teams come back, they sign it, it's a neat place. Joe and Donnie seemed very happy to be in this building."

That night Torre and Mattingly said it was wonderful being back, and that this was a great way to honor the Boss. Noted Torre proudly, "George was responsible for the best years of my life, professionally. Did we get along all the time? No. But it never lasted very long. I always felt we had a special relationship. George was so devoted to this city and these fans. There has never been a group of fans like there have been at Yankee Stadium. George put a face on this franchise that was all about winning and set very high standards to live by."

Standards that Joe Girardi tries to live up to each day. Just as Joe Torre taught him along the way.

10.

A GAME OF CHARACTER

DON'T UNDERESTIMATE THE value of talent. Joe Girardi, though, is looking for more than talent from his players. He is looking for character. The reason is simple. There are tests throughout the long baseball season, and talent can only take you so far.

Then the game becomes a question of character.

"Character," Girardi often says, "shows up every day."

Character wins. Character has to be nurtured and grown. Character and heart make a tremendous difference in this game. It's not just about the numbers in the binder. Tony LaRussa, who has the third most victories in managerial history, said it best about his amazing Cardinals during the 2011 World Series.

"Sometimes we're not good enough," LaRussa explained. "But our heart is always good enough."

That summed up his team to perfection. It helps to have the game's most feared hitter in Albert Pujols, ace Chris Carpenter, World Series MVP David Freese, and Lance Berkman red hot during the postseason, but it takes more than talent to win a championship.

Character and talent are needed to win a title.

That character and heart paid off with a stunning world championship for the Cardinals, who beat the Texas Rangers in seven games after twice being down to their last strike in Game 6 before winning 10–9 in 11 innings. The 2011 postseason was filled with close games and one surprise after another, but nothing was as shocking as the Cardinals coming back from a 10½-game deficit in the wild-card in late August to go on to win LaRussa's third World Series in 33 years of managing. Two of those championships have come over the last six years; the other was in 1989, a baseball lifetime ago with the A's.

That was the year the 24-year-old Joseph Elliott Girardi first made it to the majors with the Cubs. LaRussa's A's won 99 games that season, six more than the Cubs, and breezed through the postseason, beating the Blue Jays in five games and sweeping the Giants in the "Earthquake Series." The Giants knocked out Girardi's Cubs in five games.

Through all his years in the game, Girardi has built many friendships, prompting Northwestern coach Paul Stevens to speak about Joe in terms that are usually reserved for movie characters like Jimmy Stewart's "George Bailey" in the classic Christmas film *It's a Wonderful Life*.

"There's a lot of people at the drop of a hat would be at Joe's side to try to help him out because he has been there for a lot of people along the way," Stevens said, perhaps the greatest testimony to Girardi's strength of character.

Even though it has been more than a quarter of a century since Girardi graduated from Northwestern, every year Stevens continues to use Girardi as a reference point and a teaching tool to his players. For Girardi, it always comes back to character—that is what he is really all about—and Stevens makes sure his players understand that.

"Joe does what he believes and is not afraid to pay the price for preparation and character and standing up for what you believe in," Stevens said. "That's what we talk a lot about here. How did somebody like Joe Girardi get to where he is and why did he get there?

"You just ask little questions that, I promise you, a nine-year-old kid could answer. Are you willing to do the things that these people did to get where they are and not sell out for X, Y, or Z? And Joe hasn't done that.

"You understand that character does count and understanding who has come before you and what it means to pay respect to your elders and the ones who did it the right way like Joe does," Stevens said.

"Joe never left any stone unturned," Stevens added. "If he thought that it was going to give him an opportunity to get where he wanted to go, he wasn't going to leave it unturned. He was going to make sure firsthand it was or wasn't something. We all know your mind can be a phenomenal asset if used in the right way."

Girardi's favorite managerial saying may be the simplest one: "No excuses."

Girardi is a huge fan of Tony Dungy, not only because of the way he coached his football teams, but because of the way Dungy approaches life, his strong faith, and the fact that character counts in so many ways. Like anything else, character can be nurtured. It's not something that just shows up one day.

To help build character, Stevens has his players write letters to wounded warriors at Walter Reed Hospital each year. "We just want some of the young men there to know that we appreciate the sacrifices they've made to allow us to experience the life we have, to be able to play baseball and experience this college life," Stevens explained. "It's amazing how this group of kids I have now have responded," he said of his current crop of players.

This is Stevens' 25th season as Northwestern's head coach and 28th year in a Wildcats uniform.

"I just hope that there are more groups that were here like in the Girardi era, because if there are, we are going to have a lot more people doing a lot more good things for a lot of people besides themselves in this world, and that's something that at the end of the day definitely tugs at the heartstrings a little bit," Stevens said.

Stevens is quick to credit Ron Wellman for instilling these characteristics in his players and for their continuing to follow that path. "Ron has a lot to be proud of," Stevens said.

"I haven't heard anybody say anything negative about Joe except for one time in his career [with the Marlins], and I think he took some people to a place that I don't know that many other people could have taken a group of young kids," Stevens said of that Marlins team.

In his first year as a major league manager in 2006, Girardi took that young Marlins team from the brink of disaster and put them in playoff contention, until the team stumbled down the stretch. Girardi lost his job with the Marlins because of a contentious relationship with Marlins ownership.

Despite all that, Girardi was named the 2006 National League Manager of the Year by the Baseball Writers' Association of America. Those young Marlins were 20 games under .500 in mid-May but went 62–40 through September 11 to climb two games over .500 at 73–71 before reality hit again as the Marlins finished the season 78–84.

Girardi hollered at Marlins owner Jeffrey Loria for yelling at umpire Larry Vanover at a game on August 6, 2006. That situation helped create a schism between Girardi and ownership. After the season, Girardi was fired by the Marlins. He has never looked back in anger.

Girardi got the most he could out of those bargain-basement Marlins. As for the falling out with ownership, Girardi has never gone into great detail about the situation, saying "nothing good" could come out of it, but he has said he has grown from that experience, telling *Northwestern Magazine*, "I'm extremely thankful that I went through that experience, and you realize God's got a bigger plan than what you could've imagined."

Three years later, Girardi got the most he could out of the high-priced Yankees, as they won the World Series.

"At the end of the day, it's still about getting your players to believe in you and play for you," Stevens said. "When push comes to shove, they are willing to go that extra mile because of what you've put into them and do what they can to give back. In today's athletes, that's pretty tough."

Yes, it is, and there is no tougher division in baseball than the one in which the Yankees live, the AL East. "No one ever said this is going to be easy," Girardi said of life in the AL East with the Red Sox, Rays, Blue Jays, and Orioles. "We're in a tough division. You go out and try to win series. There are going to be bumps in the road for every team in this division. You try to keep them as short as possible and try to turn it around tomorrow."

That is essentially his philosophy of getting through the season to put the Yankees in the best position to try to win in the postseason. It worked to perfection in 2009. In 2010 the Yankees stumbled in the ALCS against the Rangers, losing in six games, and in 2011 they lost in five games to the Tigers. Just one big hit in Game 5 against the Tigers and the Yankees would have survived for a rematch with the Rangers.

Before that division series started, Girardi tried to warn everyone just how good the Tigers were, noting, "It's a complete team. They're very sound fundamentally. Their starting rotation is good, their bullpen is good, they have left-handers in their bullpen, their lineup is very good, and it's deep. This is a very good club. You don't win 95 games by accident."

Justin Verlander won both the Cy Young Award and the MVP in 2011, the first pitcher in either league to do so since A's closer Dennis Eckersley in 1992 and the first starter since Roger Clemens won both awards in 1986 while with the Red Sox.

The rain played havoc with Verlander in the 2011 postseason, but the Tigers had enough pitching to get past the Yankees, who were short on pitching. In the end, you have to wonder if the 2011 Yankees would have had enough pitching to even get to the World Series.

Brian Cashman has said that life in the AL East followed by the postseason is a lot like horse racing's Triple Crown.

"It's kind of like the Kentucky Derby, the Preakness, and Belmont.... We won the long race in terms of qualification, in terms of the wild-card or Eastern Division title, here in the regular season, now you got the shorter race in the five-game set, so your roster strengths get analyzed differently in a five-game series versus what it was over 162," Cashman said. "Then you have the seven-game stretch."

And all it takes is one slip-up in each of the races to end the season. In 2009 Girardi's Yankees never slipped, beating the Twins, Angels, and Phillies.

They slipped in each of the next two seasons. In 2011, after the Yankees' Game 4 win in Detroit, Girardi said this about going home for the decisive Game 5: "We have an opportunity. We have an opportunity to win a series. We fought all year long to have home-field advantage throughout the playoffs. Hopefully we can get it done on Thursday."

The Yankees couldn't get it done, coming up short and losing 3–2, but it wasn't because of a lack of character. The Yankees came up short because of the lack of a big hit. In the three losses to the Tigers, the Yankees were 3-for-21 with runners in scoring position.

In some ways, it was amazing that the Yankees got as far as they did in 2011, winning 97 games in the regular season, but Girardi made the patchwork rotation work as Cashman went to Plan B once the Yankees lost out on Cliff Lee, who signed with the Phillies. In 2010 the Yankees also ran out of pitching against the Rangers.

Heading into 2012, Cashman said it was all about acquiring more pitching. The game never changes; it's always about pitching, pitching, and more pitching. The Yankees are going through a challenging period as the roster continues to age with Derek Jeter at short and Alex Rodriguez at third. Jeter will turn 38 in 2012; A-Rod will be 37 and coming off a series of injuries. Closer Mariano Rivera is 42.

"We have some age," Girardi allowed. "Those are things we have to deal with, and that's why our bench players are extremely important to us."

In the 2011 season, Jorge Posada, at the age of 40, made the transition from catcher to full-time DH. Posada once replaced Girardi in the Yankees lineup, and now Girardi is the manager who had to cut Posada's ties to catching.

Baseball is forever a game that goes round and round.

There were bumps along the road in 2011 for Posada, but in the end, he delivered in the postseason. Girardi did his job by getting the most he could out of the proud Posada. Against the Tigers, Posada was one of the Yankees' best hitters, batting .429 with a .579 on-base percentage. Only Robinson Cano (.682) produced a higher slugging percentage than Posada.

Girardi said that he never lost faith in Posada's ability to hit right-handers and deliver in the big games. "We looked at what he had done against right-handers during the course of the season," Girardi noted. "We looked at Jorge's experience in these types of situations and how he's been productive. I'm sure it means a lot to him. I know it means a lot to all of us. Jorge has been through this so many times in his career and understands the magnitude of each at-bat and how to approach each at-bat. That's why we went with him." That turned out to be Posada's final season, as he retired the following January.

Stevens said Girardi has always had a way of getting the most out of his players. That is just Joe's way. "What he got out those guys, I don't know if many people would have had them in the position that they did," Stevens said, looking at Girardi's overall body of work as a manager. Girardi heads into the 2012 season with a 462–348 lifetime record as a manager over five seasons. With the Yankees he is 384–264, 120 games over .500 over four seasons.

"The people in that clubhouse do believe in him, do trust him, and do want to play for him," Stevens said. "Yes, it's the Yankees, and yes, it's an opportunity to play in one of the most storied franchises, and you are going to be at the upper end of your pay scale from top to bottom, but at the end of the day, they still want to play for him."

Stevens put it all into perspective, saying, "I do believe that Joe Girardi is a destination for players to play for, somebody who really does care for them. I just know that Joe cares about the people he is involved with. I don't think Joe likes to see anybody leave, even if they need to."

After he was named the 32nd manager in Yankees history on October 30, 2007, Girardi said that the one thing he would want people to say about him is that he cared.

Dave Eiland was Girardi's pitching coach with the Yankees when Girardi got the job and for the world championship run in 2009. Eiland's contract was not renewed by Cashman following the 2010 season. That season Eiland had to leave the Yankees from June 4 to June 29 to take care of a personal matter.

Eiland went on to work for the pitching-rich Rays the next two seasons and then got back to the majors in uniform as a pitching coach with the Royals in 2012.

Eiland loved his time working with Girardi.

"We had a great working relationship, and he cared about you as a coach and as an individual, as a person," Eiland said. "He cares about you as a human being first and your family first, and baseball follows a little farther somewhere down the line. He cared about you as much off the field as he did on the field. To me, that speaks volumes. Joe and I have remained friends. You really can't say enough good things about him.

"You would be hard-pressed to find anybody anywhere who is more prepared than he is," Eiland said. "I know he's been criticized for going to his scouting books, but his preparation is second to none. Joe uses his people. He uses his coaches. He listens. He takes input from everybody, but the decision lies with him. He digests it all and he digests it quickly, and he formulates a game plan in his head for whatever situation may arrive, and he is ready for it."

Most of all, Eiland said, Girardi trusts his people.

"He absolutely let me do my job, that's why I loved working with him, but before I ever did anything with anybody, I would always tell him my thoughts and why I did it because he is the manager," Eiland explained. "He should know. He would always give me his blessing, 'Go for it. Do it.'"

Ultimately, it all falls on the manager, so it is always the manager's final call, but Girardi gives his coaches freedom to work.

"Joe would also pick my brain about different pitches, different deliveries, and try to learn that stuff, too," Eiland said.

That industrial engineering degree is always at work, no matter the subject.

"Joe also let you speak your mind," Eiland said. "He wanted your opinion. He said, 'If you have something that is going to make me better, I want to know it. If you disagree with me, I want you to tell me.' What more could you ask for?"

Former Mets pitcher and Cubs GM Ed Lynch tells this story about Girardi the ballplayer the second time that Girardi was with the Cubs. It shows the strength of character of Girardi.

"Joe was catching for us, and there was a pitcher he had caught while with another team who was put on outright waivers by another club," Lynch said. "And I never did this with another player. I called Joe up to my office and asked him about this player because I trusted him to keep his mouth shut. Most players can't keep their mouths shut, I was a player. I know.

"So I asked Joe about this pitcher. For about five minutes Joe broke the guy down, and then he said, 'You don't want this guy, because when the going gets tough he's going to make a bad pitch because he just can't handle the pressure of a tough situation.' So, based on that, I didn't claim the guy. The next day I picked up the paper [to see if word had leaked about their conversation], and Joe never said anything. I knew Joe was a serious guy, he'd keep his mouth shut, a good solid baseball guy."

Was Girardi's scouting report accurate about the pitcher in question?

"Yes, absolutely," Lynch said.

Lynch said he could see a future manager in Girardi even back then. "Joe had a good head for the game, he was astute, he watched the game, he had a good feel for the game. He had a good relationship with pitchers," said Lynch, who is now scouting for the Blue Jays. "Pitchers are half your club, and that guy is responsible for half your club, and pitchers are basically nuts anyway."

Lynch knows. He pitched eight years in the majors.

"We're so superstitious, we're fragile, sometimes, the stupidest things get us off track, so you need a guy who can settle you down, believe in what you are doing, a guy who is not caught up in his own at-bats," he said. "That was Joe. He was a very serious young man, but I think he's got the perfect demeanor for a manager because there has to be that line between the manager and the players, there's got to be a little bit of distance there, you don't want somebody there who is going to be their friend. He had big shoes to fill, too, following Joe Torre."

Lynch understands the nuances of the game on so many levels.

"The ironic thing about catchers is people say it's the fastest way to the big leagues. Actually, it's the slowest, but once you get here, you are set," Lynch said. "You can't bring that guy up until he is ready defensively. The pitcher has to think when you are out there catching him that you really care about his outing, not your last at-bat and that you can do the job defensively."

Lynch also said he respects the way Girardi uses his relievers, never having them pitch too many days in a row. "You leave a starter out there for 150 pitches, and every talking head in America is talking about him," Lynch noted. "You pitch a [reliever] seven days in a row, nobody is talking about it. We abuse relievers like nobody's business."

Lynch also makes the excellent point that sometimes catchers get too much blame for a pitcher's failures when it simply comes down to how the pitcher executes the pitch. Pitch selection can be overrated. It is the execution of the pitch that is most important, and sometimes that gets lost because so much emphasis is put on pitch selection.

"I always felt the wrong pitch thrown correctly is better than the right pitch thrown incorrectly," Lynch said. "You never call for the hanger. Joe was good. Pitchers all had a lot of respect for him, he worked hard and showed how much he cared for his pitchers."

Character shows up every day in so many ways.

11.

TV JOE

WHEN IT COMES to baseball and TV, John Filippelli is a Hall of Famer.

Filippelli is president of production and programming at YES Network, essentially the backbone of the highly successful network. During his long career, he has been involved in the production of many of the biggest games played in baseball, in addition to the day-to-day production of baseball and other sports coverage, everything from ABC's *Wide World of Sports* to *Monday Night Football*.

He has been around baseball his entire life, growing up near Ebbets Field and working as a vendor at Yankee Stadium. He started his television career at NBC Sports in 1974. He eventually became producer for the NBC's *Game of the Week*, became a coordinating producer for the Baseball Network, was essential to FOX Sports baseball coverage, and served as a senior VP of production at ABC Sports.

He's covered it all, has a full roster of Emmy awards, and has worked with the greatest talent in the baseball world. He manages his own team of TV talent in every phase of production.

No one can give you a better read on the TV game of baseball than Filippelli, known to his friends as "Flip." When Joe Girardi entered the booth, it was Filippelli who helped guide him just as he has done with so many athletes who have moved from the field upstairs. The Yankees' current lineup of YES broadcasters include Michael Kay, Ken Singleton, Jack Curry, John Flaherty, Al Leiter, David Cone, Paul O'Neill, Bob Lorenz, Nancy Newman, Chris Shearn, and newcomer Lou Piniella.

Everyone brings his or her own strengths to the booth. What did Girardi bring to the booth?

"Joe's mind was always working, and he was fascinating," Filippelli began. "To him it was always about how do you put pressure on the other team? How do you put pressure on the other team's defense? He was great at scouting other teams, too, saying, 'To beat them, this is where you have to attack,' and he was very specific on his mode of attack. He could spot weaknesses right away and he would bring that to the air."

That perspective is so hard to come by, but in typical Girardi fashion, he threw himself into his new job.

Michael Kay has been broadcasting Yankees games the last 20 years. He is one of the best in the business and has covered Yankees managers since Billy Martin, when he worked as a beat writer for the *New York Post*. Through all the years and all the partners he has had, he has never seen anyone bring as much information to the microphone as Girardi. Kay knows Girardi from three sides of the game, on the field, in the dugout, and in the booth as a broadcast partner.

"I've never seen a guy prep more and be more buttoned up in terms of knowing exactly everything about the opponent than Joe," Kay explained. "He came into the booth and knew everything about the team the Yankees were playing and everything about the team's system and guys who were on the way up. He covered every aspect of everything you could possibly want to know; nothing ever took him by surprise.

"When the backup catcher or the third catcher came in, he had a nugget on him. It was never too much information, it was never too much prep work, the guy just worked harder than anyone I've ever seen."

That also gives you an indication of the type of information that is locked in those color-coded Girardi binders that are in the Yankees dugout for every game.

"I'm sure he takes that times 20 into a game now," Kay said of the prep work. Beyond the information, Girardi brought another huge plus to the booth.

"He brought a catcher's perspective," Filippelli said. "At the time, we had Paul O'Neill, we had David Cone, we had Kenny Singleton, Bobby Murcer, Michael and Bob Lorenz in the studio. We had no catchers, and to me, based on 40 years of doing this, it seems like there is a disproportionate amount of catchers who become good analysts, the same way there is a disproportionate number of catchers who become good managers."

Joe Torre and Joe Girardi, the last two Yankees managers to win world championships, were just that, good catchers and good analysts.

"I don't think that's by accident," Filippelli said. "I think it's because catchers see the whole field and are involved in every play, and they have to think ahead. I would tease O'Neill all the time that he would get bored in the outfield, he would be practicing his swing in the outfield."

Catchers can't be bored. Their minds and bodies are always working on every pitch. Because he threw himself into his work with such enthusiasm and passion, Girardi found a new home above the field, in the broadcast booth, even though the competitive spirit still burned. It was still baseball, all the fun of baseball, all the strategy, but it was all pressure-free on a daily basis. It was almost like going back to the sandlots for Joe.

"I loved that job," Girardi said. "That job, you love everything that you love to do. You are around baseball. You are preparing. You are watching the game. You are talking about the game. But wins and losses don't mean anything. So you go home."

On TV, it's just a game. That game doesn't tear your heart out. There isn't the same joy of success or thrill of victory, of course, and that was the downside to being on TV and not in the dugout. But for Girardi it was the perfect break he needed to be away from the game and still be immersed in the game.

After he retired as a player, following the 2003 season with the Cardinals, Girardi did work for ESPN Radio during the NL Division Series, and that opened the door to YES. In addition to being a game analyst for YES Network, Girardi won an Emmy for the *Kids on Deck* series. In 2007 he rejoined YES, working as an analyst after his Marlins managerial experience. By then, with that experience of managing in the major leagues behind him, he brought even more perspective to the booth.

And he loved the view, too. Girardi has watched the game from three totally different perspectives. As a catcher, he was the only fielder who faced the field from the batter's point of view. In that way, his viewpoint was much like the home-plate camera, only the foul balls really hurt.

As a coach and now a manager, Girardi watches the game from the dugout: life along the rail. In the world of television, Girardi got the panoramic view of the game, the bird's-eye, super slow-mo view. From that vantage point, it's a totally different game.

"I'll tell you what, the game looks so much different from up there than it does down here," Girardi said as he stood in the visiting dugout at Tropicana Field during the last week of the 2011 season. "You see the whole field, you see how players move, and you see different angles. It just looks different. As a player, you are always at this level, field level.

"I really love the view from up there."

You get the sense that when his managing days end, and as his family grows up, some day Girardi will land back in the broadcasting booth. He is a natural, has the type of information fans love to hear, and in TV, Girardi also allowed his personality to take center stage.

Girardi loved the view, but make no mistake, in 2007 he missed the competitive fire of the game that he had as a player, that he had as a coach, as manager of the Marlins. In 2007 Girardi also worked with FOX during the regular season and postseason. His TV career was on a rapid rise. But it wasn't as much fun as managing.

"I knew he wanted to get back in the dugout," Kay said. "I told him once, 'Joe, why would you want to get back to the dugout? This job pays tremendous money. You are really good at it, and you are not just good at it on a local level doing Yankees games. You are eventually going to be on FOX and you are going to be one of the main guys. That's how good you are.'

"He said to me, 'Thank you, but they don't keep score up here.'"

Girardi needs that competitive jolt to complete him. He needs to keep score. Broadcasters keep score of the game, but keeping score of broadcasters is really is so subjective, and Girardi picked that up right away, telling Kay, "Whether or not we do well is totally subjective, one person could think we do great, another person could think we were terrible, there is no scoreboard that tells you definitively if you were great or terrible. I miss that competition."

For someone who kept score his entire life, that was a difficult adjustment. Kay said at that moment, "I knew he was going back to managing."

From the beginning of Girardi's broadcasting career, Filippelli knew he had found a real talent.

"Girardi was a very good broadcaster, and he would have been even better if he stayed," Filippelli said. "Listen, he got a network interested in him inside of two seasons. He was on FOX, remember. He took it so seriously."

The irony is that by taking broadcasting so seriously and doing such a good job at it, people got to see the other side of Joe Girardi. The Joe Girardi that the press rarely sees. Here is an inside look from Kay.

"The difference was he was much more fun-loving and goofy and looser as a television guy," Kay explained. "He and O'Neill were great together. Joe was great on the air, and he prepped as if he were managing against that team. O'Neill was great on the air, and didn't prep at all."

Opposites attract. Even in the broadcast booth. Kay remembers how it went: "Joe would look at me, and say about Paul, 'The guy doesn't even bring a pencil up to the booth.' Joe would keep score during the game, and he'd say to O'Neill, 'I brought you a pen, Paul.' They couldn't have been more different in their approach, and they were really both very good on the air. I think that Joe, in the booth, was closer to the player that he was, and O'Neill in the booth was completely different than the player he was. By the sixth inning, O'Neill was saying, 'These games are so long.' And he was ready to go. If he did three games in a row, he was exhausted."

In many ways, O'Neill, as a broadcaster, is this generation of Yankees fans' Phil Rizzuto, the broadcaster buddy who is hanging out watching the game with you.

Together, Girardi and O'Neill offered great team chemistry. The Girardi-O'Neill Show was all in good fun. "The two of them truly loved each other," Kay said. "Joe would have been a big star if he stayed in the booth. I don't think he is going to be like Tony LaRussa, managing when he is 66 years old, I think he is going to end up back in the booth someday, yet he somehow has to satisfy his competitive jones."

Managing gives you that competitive fix, but it is an incredible grind.

"I always worry about Joe because he seemed happier, looser, and he had more dark hair when he was in the booth than as a manager," Kay said. "I've asked him a number of times over the years, 'Are you having a good time as a manager? Are you having fun?'

"He'd say to me, 'I love this.'"

Kay would counter, "It looks like you are miserable."

But that's Joe. "He's so intense, I don't know if he enjoys the rare chance he is having as being the manager of the New York Yankees," Kay added. "I know he says he does. The thing that bothers me the most about being the manager is that all the writers don't like him. I shouldn't paint with a broad stroke. But they don't think he's a good guy. I spend my time telling them, 'Joe is not just a good guy, he's a great guy.' But he never lets that side of himself show as a manager. I don't think he trusts many people."

That is an astute observation from Kay. Girardi keeps the media at arm's length as a manager. There is a clear line that he will not cross—even with his friends, like Kay, in the media. He will take a bullet for the players. He does not offer information about his team. All the information he brought to the booth is pretty much locked away as a manager only to be used by his team. It is information for his team, not information for the media and not for the fans. Girardi wants to give his team an edge so the less information out there about his team, the better it is for his team. In New York there are more reporters than any other market, and they all want information. But Girardi closely guards even the slightest bit of information. That is always going to be his way as manager of the Yankees.

Remember, it was those scouting reports that Girardi brought to the booth that really caught Filippelli's eye. Filippelli always recognized Girardi's true calling to be a manager, not a broadcaster. "It wasn't the generic stuff," Filippelli explained, "like a starting pitcher has to go deep into the game, he went far deeper than that, and I would say to him all the time: 'I think you are an exceptional broadcaster, but I think your calling is as a manager.'"

Girardi got managing offers while in the booth, but he was waiting for the right offer from the Yankees. The booth was a great place to keep in tune with the game and to keep tabs on the Yankees.

Filippelli hired Girardi because Girardi was working the 2003 NL playoffs, and Filippelli just happened to hear him broadcast a game.

"I was driving in a car, taking one of my kids back to school, and he was working radio—one of the Braves playoff games. I'm in my car listening to the game, and I said, 'Who is this analyst? He's terrific. I want to hire the guy on the spot.' He's saying, 'The pitcher is throwing inside so he can go outside, this is a total setup pitch…. He's going to come back now. He's going to chase. They'll hit and run here…they'll open up the hole…they'll take advantage of their speed.'

"He was saying it all, no clichés, just his observations, and they were pouring out of him. He was awesome. I never heard an analyst have them pouring out of him like that.' He was taking you right into the dugout, and I loved that. Every time something would come into my head, he was giving you the answer. I thought he was that good.

"But I had no idea it was Joe. Finally, they did a reset, and it said Joe Girardi.' I said right then and there, 'I'm hiring this guy.'"

Once Girardi got to the Yankees booth, Girardi's personality began to shine. Yes, as a manager he plays everything close to the vest. He does not like to give out any information that he believes will help the opposing team. In the booth, there was nothing to hide; he had the information and he had fun with it. O'Neill and Girardi, Filippelli said, "became like *The Odd Couple*. Joe had a sense of humor, and he knew his place," Filippelli said.

Girardi also brought a human element to the booth that really made an impact on Kay. "When there were kids who came in to visit the booth who might have been disabled or sick, Joe would be great with them, but there were times he would have to turn away because he started to cry. You never see this side of this guy. I wish that side of it would come out."

Girardi loves to eat, too. Kay admits to having a "terrible palate" and limits the type of food he eats. He's not exactly a Food Network kind of guy. Kay has never eaten eggs, tomatoes, or mayonnaise. "Joe didn't like the way I ate, the way I lost weight on different diets," Kay explained.

Girardi said to Kay of the diets, "I don't do that stuff."

"Yeah," Kay responded, "but you work out two hours a day."

"He would beg me to eat egg whites, he would tell me to put Tabasco on them, and it's a great way to get protein. I wouldn't do it," Kay said.

Managers who go to the booth usually don't second-guess the managers on the field. There is sensitivity to the profession, not a lot of hot sauce.

Girardi didn't second-guess.

"He never second-guessed, he first-guessed," Filippelli explained. "Which I thought was brilliant on his part. He liked Joe Torre, he played for him, he coached for him, and he wasn't going to second-guess him. He first-guessed.

"If I go down to the clubhouse now, is it a different relationship? Yes," Filippelli said. "Is it a relationship that I cherish less? No, not at all. I still see him socially. His family life means everything to him. Joe has such strength of conviction, like when he pitched the three guys in the [2009 postseason]. That was his best option. And it worked. He's a guy of conviction, and I greatly respect him for that. Some people call it stubbornness, I call it conviction."

A manager must have conviction. He must have the ability to sell a player on what is best for the team. Remember, Girardi's dad held many jobs to take care of his family. The son knows what he has to sell and when he has to sell it.

"He has the players' backs," Filippelli said. "He believes in the sanctity of the clubhouse. He's not a PR machine. He's old-school. Unfortunately, we are in a media age where everything is documented, YouTubed, and blogged—everybody is a documentarian. ESPN redefined things. More and more platforms keep popping up. The media demands have never been stronger. You have never been more in the public eye. Sometimes I think that is Joe's toughest challenge. He can handle the players, he will do what he needs to do to give the Yankees the best chance to win, and I respect that about him."

Girardi is still on the air at YES with *The Joe Girardi Show*, and he clearly enjoys his time there with Kay. But inside information is not traded by Girardi with Kay or anyone else.

"His press sessions are like pulling teeth," Kay noted. "He never shows what a warm guy he is."

That family guy is under the pinstriped uniform.

"A think a lot of people in sports pay lip service, saying, 'I want to be with my family,'" noted Kay. "Then they retire and they play golf all the time and they are never with their family. Joe Girardi legitimately loves his family, every single second away from the ballpark he spends with his family. Even when he is at the ballpark, he spends time hitting balls to Dante, he's spending time with Serena. He loves being with his family. I've seen very few husbands who worship their wives as much as he loves Kim. The way he works at it, the way he talks about it, it's unbelievable."

Joe and Kim are a true partnership—even when it comes to baseball.

Noted Kay, "She once told me a story that when he was in the minor leagues she would pitch socks to him in the house and she said something to him like, 'I hope you're a great defensive catcher.'"

Evidently, Kim Girardi is a pretty good baseball scout, too.

Kay can see all sides of Joe Girardi. He made it clear that he does not blame the media for not seeing the softer side, the other side, of Girardi, "because he doesn't let them see it, which is really disappointing. I think the year the Yankees won the championship with Joe as manager, he was closer to what he was in the booth. I guess people spoke to him, but it's now back to what it was before. You got to really get his trust before you get his trust."

When Kay does *The Joe Girardi Show* now, he tries to bring out Girardi's personality. "Sometimes I succeed," Kay explained. "But the thing that really derails it for me is that he is never giving away a state secret. As close as we are, he has never told me anything off the record of what is happening."

Girardi and Kay are close.

Girardi's charity foundation is called Catch 25, which is dedicated to providing support to families and individuals across the country who have been challenged with Alzheimer's, ALS, cancer, and fertility issues, as noted in the Yankees' media guide. Catch 25 provides assistance through scholarships, financial aid, and emotional support where needed. Girardi hosts the annual "Remember When, Remember Now" benefit along with Kay. There is a bond between the two men.

The term "off the record" is often used by managers, GMs, players, and club officials as a way to get information without that information being pointed directly to the source.

"Joe will never say to me, 'By the way, this is happening...'"
Kay noted. "Even if it is going to come out and I might look bad
not knowing it, he won't tell me. Even if he knows that by the time
the show runs it's going to be obsolete, because he does not want
anybody to know anything. The guy was at my wedding, and he
would never tell me, 'By the way, this guy is going on the DL today.'
Even if it is happening in an hour, he will not say it."

That is so Joe Girardi. He is never going to be the guy who tells
a writer, "Listen, you didn't hear it from me, but..."

Kay's indoctrination into covering the Yankees was with Billy
Martin as a manager when Kay worked for the *New York Post*.

"My career was made by Billy Martin because he would tell me
stuff that was going to happen three days before it happened," Kay
explained. "And I'm closer with Joe than I am with Billy, but Billy
would give me stuff, and Joe never has. Joe Girardi just does not
give anybody any story, and he never will."

Girardi understands his role as Yankees manager is to protect
the players and get the most out of them using his style of managing. He understood that his role as a catcher was to get the most
out of the pitcher, and that hitting was secondary. He understood
what he brought to the broadcast booth.

As Filippelli pointed out, "He understands the role of the
broadcaster. He worked with Michael; he worked with Kim
[Jones] when he worked with YES, so to him, we're an extension
of family. He is one of the most loyal people I've ever met in my
life. That is at his core. That's what he is about. I think there are
times when loyalty is misunderstood, and I think it was his first
year, here [as a manager]. He was trying to protect players or not
to give too much information out. At the end of the day, he
believes his job is to protect the players and the front office. He's
not a finger-pointer."

"The only time I've ever seen him get chapped is when he thinks someone is not giving him their best effort or playing stupid baseball."

Girardi has sent that message to his players and has helped them reach their potential, especially Robinson Cano at second base. There were times when Girardi has had to lean on Cano when he first started managing the club, and Cano, who had an MVP-like season in 2011, has grown tremendously as a player and a person because of that experience.

On the air, Filippelli said, he never saw Girardi lose his temper. "Never, even privately," Filippelli explained. "Even private discussions were always couched with comments like, 'You're in charge. You're my boss.' It all went back to principle with him. His core values. It's almost his default setting—everything goes back to his core values. Once you understand what those are about him, everything else makes sense."

YES it does, everything makes perfect sense.

12.

PASSION PLAY

RAY NEGRON TOOK the road less traveled to forge a career in baseball with the Yankees. He is a community advisor with the team, working closely with players, management, and the local community. If a Yankee is making an appearance to speak to a seriously ill child at a hospital, Negron is usually the one who sets up the meeting. He's also a best-selling author of a children's book series, and his animated feature film *Henry & Me*, starring Richard Gere, is scheduled for release in spring of 2012.

Negron has been around the major league game in a variety of jobs, all because he got caught writing graffiti on the walls of Yankee Stadium back in 1973 when he was a teenager. He wasn't caught by just anyone; he was caught by George M. Steinbrenner.

"I was spray-painting 'NY' on the wall," Negron, always a Yankees fan, began. "I loved the Yankees. Mr. Steinbrenner caught me red-handed. He put me in the holding cell at the old Yankee Stadium, not the renovated Yankee Stadium that was reopened in 1976—this was the old, old Yankee Stadium. George had a security guard with him, and he caught me. It was me and several others. My cousins and brothers got away, I got caught. I was on the side wall, and they were on top of me right away. George didn't waste any time, he had me put in lockup.

"All of a sudden he came back 20 minutes later and said, 'Give me the kid,' and next thing you know, they took me to the Yankees locker room, and he had Pete Sheehy give me a uniform and he told Pete, 'He's got damages that he's got to work for.' And that night I was the batboy for the New York Yankees."

Pete Sheehy was the legendary equipment manager with the Yankees who started working for the club back in the days of Babe Ruth, so Negron had a living link to Yankees legends standing right in front of him. Overnight, Negron went from a kid causing trouble to wearing pinstripes and running errands for the likes of Thurman Munson and Bobby Murcer.

It was a Yankees dream that came true. Steinbrenner gave the youngster a second chance, and Negron made the most of it. At first, Negron thought he would just be around the club a few days. Forty years later, he is still around the Yankees on an everyday basis, and he cherished all the years he spent with George Steinbrenner.

"The Boss saved my life," said Negron, who went on to become a second-round pick of the Pittsburgh Pirates. "I was a shortstop. And when I got released, George brought me back to the Yankees, first as a batting practice pitcher. When I proved I couldn't do that, he decided to buy video equipment and had me learn how to use it. I was the very first video guy that the Yankees ever had. The Yankees were the very first team to bring video operations to the team.

"I would video the hitters and the pitchers."

George Steinbrenner came to baseball with a football mentality, and he wanted to bring some of those day-to-day football operations to the game of baseball. He always wanted his coaches and players to do more. Steinbrenner wanted to shake things up in the clubhouse and wanted any edge he could get for his team.

Negron said it was Steinbrenner who also kick-started strength-training for baseball players in the mid-1970s. "George started the weight room," Negron explained. "The equipment he brought to baseball was Nautilus equipment, and that is why they called it the 'Nautilus Room.' Soon, everybody followed."

As for the video work, this was nothing like today's sophisticated video operations, where players can instantly watch their at-bats on their iPads and go frame by frame to make an adjustment. The Yankees have a state-of-the-art video room located directly behind their dugout, steps away from the indoor batting cages. The Yankees hitters and batting coach Kevin Long make the most of that setup. Negron's equipment was from another generation.

"That was reel-to-reel video," Negron explained. "My job was to do the video work and to clean the Nautilus room."

Through the years, Negron became friends with countless ballplayers and crossed the generations of Yankees stars. He puts Girardi up there with some of the biggest names in Yankees history because of the way Girardi has handled himself as a person and the way he has handled the Yankees clubhouse as a manager.

"He has taken care of that clubhouse like no other Yankees manager ever has," Negron said. "Remember, Joe Torre, there were guys who liked him and guys who didn't like him. You can go all the way back to Billy Martin, and it's the same thing. There were guys who liked him and there were guys who didn't like him, period.

"The one thing about Girardi is that he goes to bat for every player," Negron said, repeating the two words slowly to make sure his point is crystal clear: "Every player. That's the phenomenal thing about this guy."

It's usually not that way in Yankees history.

"Billy didn't like Reggie," explained Negron, who managed to build strong friendships with both Billy Martin and Reggie Jackson, the only person to do so. "I don't care what anybody says, Joe Torre was not crazy about Alex Rodriguez. However, I've never seen that in Girardi. He's just a good guy.

"He wants to win, but he also wants the guys to be happy in that clubhouse. He genuinely goes out of his way to make sure all the players are happy in that clubhouse. He makes sure that in the spring he has one or two days where the guys hang out together, and that helps form a bond that lasts throughout the season. Joe goes out of his way not only to make the players feel good about what they are doing, but what all the workers around the club are doing, the clubhouse guys, everyone. And, in turn, everybody wants to go through the wall for that man."

Brett Gardner is one of those players. Girardi has nurtured Gardner, and now the young outfielder has become a vital weapon for the Yankees at a bargain-basement price, leading the American League in stolen bases in 2011 with 49, along with Oakland's Coco Crisp.

Gardner's 103 steals within his first three years as a Yankee are the most by a Yankee since Ben Chapman stole 113 bases within the first three years of his Yankee debut 82 years ago, according to the Elias Sports Bureau. Over his first four seasons, Gardner has 135 stolen bases in 163 attempts, and his 82.8 percent success rate ranks fourth among active players with at least 100 stolen-base attempts. In the five-game loss to the Tigers in the 2011 ALDS, Gardner came up big, batting .412.

Girardi has helped develop those skills in Gardner, and Gardner is appreciative of the work and the care the manager has given him.

"Joe is so great to play for; he is very competitive and wants to win at all costs," Gardner explained. "I think he does a really good job of communicating with his players. He gets us fired up, he gets us ready to play, and he's a guy we like playing for. You saw that fire when he played. He's just been so great, and I hope he's the only manager I ever play for."

That says it all.

As the Yankees transition to a younger team, as younger talent migrates through the system thanks to the work of vice president of amateur scouting Damon Oppenheimer, Girardi's ability to get the most out of his younger players will be one of the key issues to future success. Rookie pitcher Ivan Nova won 16 games for the Yankees in 2011. Setup man David Robertson could be a closer for most other clubs. The Yankees are getting younger under Girardi.

Yankees broadcaster John Sterling notes the strengths of Girardi that will play well over the long haul, saying, "Joe and I get along extremely well. After all, I was really buddies with Joe Torre, he's really a friend, but I think Joe Girardi is terrific, too. He doesn't like to tell the media too much. I ask him in kind of different ways since we meet every day for this show. I think as a manager he is expert at resting players. A lot of managers and coaches, in all sports, they're afraid of their jobs, and they keep playing their players all the time because they don't want to be knocked, they're covering their behind. They don't want to be knocked for not using their best players. Joe Girardi knows how long a year it is, so he does a lot of things to help the players. He rests them. He puts them at DH. He's just not afraid. He has lineups sometimes, I say, 'My goodness! What a lineup!' I told him that one day, and he laughed, but he does it so he takes care of his players. I think he is a great seasoned manager. And the proof of the pudding is that here is a ballclub that has no, outside of CC [Sabathia], no consistent starting pitching, and they had the best record in the American League [in 2011], and they play in the American League East. If you knock the guy and fire the guy when the team doesn't play well—well, he should get kudos when they do play well. I think he has done a fabulous job."

Negron goes so far as to say this about Girardi: "I'd take a bullet for him, the only other manager that I would take a bullet for, and that's because I loved him like a father, was Billy Martin."

When Girardi was first hired by the Yankees, Hank Steinbrenner compared Girardi to Martin, saying, "I think Girardi is going to end up being one of the greatest managers in the history of the game. That's my gut feeling. He reminds me of Billy Martin—without the baggage."

When Girardi was a player with the Yankees, Negron got to see firsthand how he treated people, and it made a lasting impression. He then tells this compelling story:

"Joe Girardi finds out that a guy who had been shot around the corner from Yankee Stadium was now paralyzed but was running a Little League from his wheelchair, and what does Joe do? He goes around the corner after a game, gives a clinic to the kids. And that's all they were expecting, for Joe to come over and teach them something about baseball, but as he's leaving he goes over to the gentleman in the wheelchair and hands him a personal check. 'This is for your league,' he says. 'I hope it can help a little bit. I wish I could give you more.'

"Right there in the neighborhood, Joe Girardi came up big for the neighborhood," Negron explained. "There was no media around, no anything, nobody even knew."

Quietly, Girardi did what he could at the time.

"This was a guy in a wheelchair who just wanted to get the kids off the street, and Girardi found out about it and did something about it," Negron said. "This guy is so humble and so sweet with his time, as far as helping people."

As Negron began to develop his animated film *Henry & Me*, he had a part for a young girl, and he pictured Girardi's daughter in the role. It turns out that Serena Girardi is a natural actor and quickly won over the producers and director in her role as an angel in the film, an angel who helps guide the main character, a child named Jack through a baseball version of *Alice in Wonderland* that

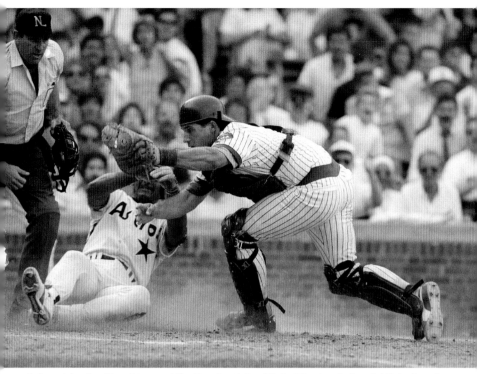

Cubs catcher Joe Girardi tags out the Houston Astros' Rafael Ramirez in the eighth inning of a 10–9 comeback win for Chicago at Wrigley Field on August 29, 1989. The Cubs won in 10 innings after climbing back from a 9–0 deficit.

As a member of the expansion Colorado Rockies, Girardi lashes a single against the Florida Marlins on June 19, 1995, at Denver's Coors Field.

With the Yankees, Girardi watches his RBI triple off of Atlanta Braves ace Greg Maddux in the third inning of Game 6 of the 1996 World Series. The hit scored Paul O'Neill for the first Yankees run of the game.

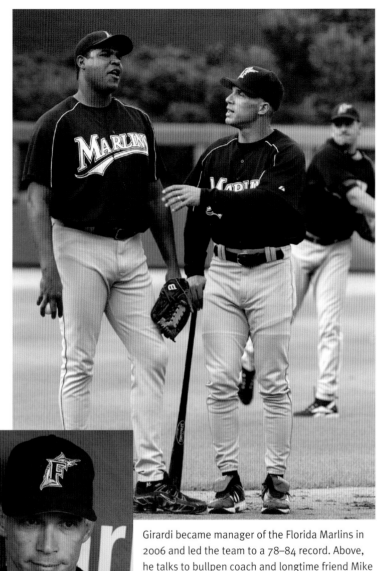

Girardi became manager of the Florida Marlins in 2006 and led the team to a 78–84 record. Above, he talks to bullpen coach and longtime friend Mike Harkey before a game against the Philadelphia Phillies on September 22, in Philadelphia. Girardi was fired October 3, 2006, a move that had been expected after his rift with owner Jeffrey Loria boiled over in an on-field confrontation.

Girardi sits with his wife, Kim, after being introduced as the New York Yankees' new manager during a press conference on November 1, 2007, at Yankee Stadium.

Girardi answers questions at a news conference after a game against the Tampa Bay Rays on July 9, 2011, at Yankee Stadium while his daughter, Lena, leans on his shoulder.

Girardi helps his then-six-year-old son, Dante, put on his shin guards as his eight-year-old daughter Serena (right) plays with one-year-old Lena on the field after the team's spring training workouts on February 15, 2008, at Legends Field in Tampa, Florida.

Girardi plays with his daughter, Lena, on the field after the Yankees' come-from behind 9–8 win over the Toronto Blue Jays at Yankee Stadium on June 5, 2008.

Yankees bench coach Tony Pena (left), hitting coach Kevin Long (center), and manager Joe Girardi talk together in the dugout in the fourth inning of a game against the Cleveland Indians on April 18, 2009, at Yankee Stadium.

Girardi stands with Yankees third baseman Alex Rodriguez (left) on the field before a game against the Boston Red Sox at Yankee Stadium on July 6, 2008.

Nine-year-old Dante Girardi (right), son of Joe Girardi (No. 28), watches the Yankees take batting practice with his dad before a spring training game against the Toronto Blue Jays in Dunedin, Florida, on March 18, 2011.

features meetings with Babe Ruth, Lou Gehrig, and many other Yankees legends.

Serena, whose character is named Sissy, has perhaps the two most heartfelt words in the film when she is asked if she misses her parents and responds soulfully, "Every day."

"Richard Gere is great in this film, but Serena ended up being one of the best actors in the show," Negron explained. "She made me look like a genius."

Girardi also had some lines in the film and said, "I had to do them a lot more than she did. She is really comfortable doing this."

"This is what I want to do," Serena, 12, said of acting. "I've always loved it. I'm the only one in my family who likes to act."

When a clip of the film was played at Yankee Stadium during the 2011 season that included a line from Serena, Girardi admitted, "It gave me a little tear in my eye, hearing her voice."

Henry & Me's director Barrett Esposito said of Serena, "I really believe she is a natural. She gets it. You work with a lot of actors, but you want the actors to understand what you are trying to do, and she gets it. We discussed the scene beforehand. She knew exactly where she was in the scene, where she had come from, where she was going, and she understood what her role was. All you really want to do is make people feel comfortable and at ease and just pretend that nothing is out there and really just try to get into the character. That's what I try to do with all the actors."

In many ways, Esposito's job is similar to managing a team.

"Serena is a ray of sunshine, and Joe has fully supported this project," noted producer Joe Castellano, adding of Girardi, "Here he is dealing with all these big-time baseball personalities and then seeing him deal with his daughter, it's good to see him in both roles, just to see him switch gears. I guess the players are all big kids, too."

There is no doubt about that.

"It's her passion," Girardi added. "I want my kids to do what they love because I've found that you work a lot harder in something that you really love to do. If you have a passion for it, it's not work."

Even though it looks like torturous work when the camera gets a close-up of Girardi along the rail in the Yankees dugout, Girardi is convinced that managing is his passion. But it's not just about managing the game. It's about managing people.

"I think what's important to me are preparation, accountability, trust, players not only trusting me, but trusting each other," he explained.

As for his players, he said, "I care about them as men first."

Girardi is often at the ballpark with his children. It's a family place. Dante is often taking batting practice or fielding grounders. When Serena needed braces, Girardi also got braces to show his support for her.

"I made a deal with my daughter Serena that if she had to get braces, I would go through it with her," Girardi explained. "Kim had always encouraged me to get braces to straighten my teeth out, and I never did. I said I was a player and I always had an excuse, but Serena was not real excited about getting hers. So I said, 'I'll tell you what, if you get 'em, I'll get 'em, and we'll go through it together.' I'm done with them. She'll probably have to put them back on later when she gets to her teenage years."

What kind of impression did that make on Serena?

"It meant a lot," Serena said, "because he promised me that when I was like five. He kept his promise, he didn't say, 'Oh I was just kidding.' He's always going to keep his word and be there for me."

It's the little things. Life is always about the little things. Consider this story about one Yankees 2009 World Series ring.

An employee associated with the club lost his job after that 2009 world championship season. That employee did not get a

World Series ring, while many others who worked in his area were presented with rings. It is common practice that when players get traded during a championship season, they still get rings from their former clubs, but this person did not get a ring. Girardi eventually learned that this worker never got a ring, a ring that would have meant so much to him. Girardi quietly went to the upper levels of Yankees management and told the appropriate people that he thought this person should be presented with a ring for all his hard work that season. When Girardi was told that a certain number of rings were distributed in that area, and there was nothing that could be done at this point, he stepped up to the plate and said he would purchase a ring for that person.

At that point, an adjustment was made; the team made sure that person got his World Series ring. The right thing was done.

Will there be more rings in Girardi's future?

That 2009 World Series victory ended a long postseason losing streak for the Yankees. Since blowing the 3–0 lead to the Red Sox in the 2004 ALCS, the Yankees did not win a playoff series until Girardi's Yankees swept the Twins in the 2009 ALDS on their way to that World Series title.

Before Girardi took over for Torre in 2008, Girardi had only one 78–84 season under his managing belt and 1,989 fewer wins than Torre. He's already come a long way in four short years of managing the Yankees, but there are still many more to go.

Yankees fans expect the Yankees to be in the World Series every season. That's life in New York. It is a city of great drama and great expectations.

Girardi's approach to the postseason is basic and realistic. "I think anyone who gets into the postseason is as dangerous as anyone else, that's the bottom line," he said. "You can run into a couple of hot starters, and that's it. My first objective is to make sure our team is ready and healthy to go when the playoffs begin.

Health is always the biggest issue, and I'm trying to make sure that my guys are fresh, too."

That is the bottom line. The Yankees will always be about winning world championships, and Girardi wears No. 28 now to constantly remind himself of the ultimate goal. But he is realistic about how tough it is to win a title.

"My true passion," Girardi explained, "is being on the field with my players and trying to get the most out of them."

Negron is amazed at Girardi's passion for the game and his family.

"I've never seen someone who is so family-oriented and yet so strong as an individual and as a manager," Negron explained. "We will never see this animal again. Every time he sees me, he knows I am hitting him from a charity standpoint because he knows who I am and he has never ever said, 'No.' And I'm a pain in the neck. I am relentless, and he has never said no as a player, a coach, or a manager.

"Let me put it to you like this: I have Joe right up there with the Boss, Billy, Bobby Murcer, Reggie, and Thurman Munson. Those are special, special people. It will be 40 years with the Yankees for me, and in those 40 years, those six guys are tops in my Yankees life."

That is quite a Monument Park of his own Negron has built, and his words speak volumes for Girardi.

"Look at his body, look how he works out, he is an example to his players," Negron said. "He works out like a madman. We have a very professional relationship, and I sincerely love the guy for who he is, what he is, his heart, and his soul."

13.

RUNNING ON AIR

THIS WAS BEFORE Joe Girardi won three World Series in four years with the Yankees as a player. This was before his triple against Greg Maddux and the Braves in the third inning of Game 6 of the 1996 World Series became the hit that sent the Yankees on their way to their amazing run under Joe Torre with four world championships in five years.

In his four years with those Yankees, the club played 14 World Series games and won 12 of them. That's winning.

This was one of those quiet, behind-the-scenes clubhouse situations where Girardi proved to be a leader for Torre's Yankees in the most valuable of ways, in a way that no one really knew or talked about. But Tino Martinez knew how much Girardi meant to him and meant to the Yankees from the first day that he arrived with the Yankees in spring training.

On November 20, 1995, Girardi was traded from the Rockies to the Yankees for right-handed pitcher Mike DeJean. It was a busy time for the Yankees. Girardi's former Cubs manager Don Zimmer pushed Torre to make a deal for Girardi, and that's what new GM Bob Watson did. A few weeks later, the Yankees made another important trade, sending third baseman Russ Davis and left-hander Sterling Hitchcock to the Seattle Mariners for Martinez, right-hander Jim Mecir, and right-handed reliever Jeff Nelson. Nelson and his slider became an incredible weapon for the Yankees. Over his next five seasons with the Yankees, Nelson pitched 293⅓ innings and struck out 313 batters, and you can be sure most of them were cursing Nellie's slider on the way back to the dugout.

Those two trades made a tremendous impact on the team. Martinez was about to become a first-base force for the Yankees, but first he had to find his confidence as a player in a new city, and that is where Girardi came into the picture. This is what the fans didn't see.

"People really didn't realize how tough it was for me to come here to New York and replace Don Mattingly," Martinez began, telling the story of what Girardi meant to that 1996 club that was trying to find itself under a new manager after four years under Buck Showalter.

Remember, Torre had yet to win any championships in his career as a player or a manager. This was before the six pennants and four World Series titles.

"Joe Girardi really helped me get through it," Martinez said of those difficult early days. "Joe had a similar situation replacing Mike Stanley, a popular guy."

Yes, he did, but it was not quite the same as replacing a Yankees legend like Mattingly. For Girardi there were some difficult moments, like the time Girardi got booed at the Yankees Welcome Home Dinner that first season.

Stanley hit .285 his four years with the Yankees. Once you get booed at a Welcome Home Dinner, that toughens you up for the long haul. That was tough on Girardi, and so were some of the comments made by fans that he should go back to Colorado, but Girardi's inner strength would not let him fail or lose focus.

Martinez could have easily faltered under the pressure to replace the Yankees icon, Donnie Baseball. Girardi would not let him falter.

That is Girardi's gift.

Other players could hit with power. Over 15 seasons, Girardi compiled 4,535 plate appearances and hit all of 36 home runs. The engineer in him could never quite figure out the proper load to get power in his swing. He was a classic singles hitter with a bit of a clunky swing. Hitting never came easy to him. Girardi busted his tail every day just to put together a workable swing that produced an overachieving .267 lifetime batting average.

Over those 15 seasons, Girardi managed 1,100 hits, a nice round number. Of those 1,100 hits, 36 were home runs, 26 were triples, and 186 went for doubles. Only 36 home runs in 4,535 plate appearances. He hit 852 singles.

That's simply who he was as a hitter.

In 2006, the year he became a major league manager with the Marlins, Girardi told this story to the *New York Times* about his offensive struggles as a young player.

"One night in my second year in the big leagues, I came home after a game," Girardi explained. "We were living in a small townhouse at the time, and my wife Kim came downstairs and said, 'Why aren't you sleeping up here?'

"And I said to her, 'I'm playing so bad I'm not worthy to sleep in the same bed as you.' I mean, it's just crazy what goes through your mind."

That is Joe Girardi being tough on himself—forget about the fans being tough on him.

A revealing comment like that makes it easier to understand where Girardi is coming from every time you hear him talk after a Yankees game now about how difficult it is to hit in the major leagues. You begin to understand where he is coming from because this was a player who struggled mightily to hit major league pitching, a player who worked day and night to become a lifetime .267 singles hitter.

The game is hard. And then when you get booed at a Welcome Home Dinner by the Yankees' most loyal fans and you realize what you're up against, it's even harder, but none of that stopped Girardi from trying to help other players. That was his gift.

Girardi had the defensive skills a catcher needed, the leadership, and the mindset to carry others through tough times. That's what he gave to new teammate Tino Martinez.

"At that point in my career Joe was always giving me positive feedback," Martinez explained with eyes wide open, still amazed at the impact Girardi had on him. "He may have been struggling at the same time, but he was always concerned about me, saying, 'Hey, stay positive. You're a good player.'

"I'll never forget that," Martinez said. "I had just met him, but he was in my corner all the way. He was a National Leaguer, so I really didn't know him, and I was with Seattle, but man, that first year together, we hit it off and became real good friends, and that really helped me stay positive to get through my early rough stretch."

There is no statistic to measure that kind of help. Not UZR. Not WAR. Not OPS.

There is no computer module for that kind of leadership. There is a feeling in the heart, though, that tells you what that kind of support means to a player. Having a teammate like Joe Girardi and the support he offered, paid off for Martinez in many ways. It paid off for the Yankees. Martinez might never have been the Yankees success he became without Girardi's emotional backing.

Girardi's Yankees career got off to a slow start, too, but that didn't matter.

He hit only .243 his first month. Martinez got off to a similar start, batting .244. Slowly though, Martinez got better as the season progressed. The lefty first baseman hit .284 in May of 1996, .314 in June, .326 in July, and .343 in August.

Giving him encouragement all along was the catcher, Girardi.

In August of that first Yankees season, Martinez hit seven home runs and drove in 24 runs, his most productive month. He was on his way to a great Yankees career. The Yankees were on their way to a dynasty that hasn't been seen in baseball for quite some time.

Now when Martinez thinks of Girardi the manager, he immediately understands what Girardi brings to the table and how it is easy to play for Girardi because he is so supportive. That is how you get the most out of your players on an everyday basis. The players have to believe the manager is completely behind them. There has to be no doubt.

"That's why Joe is a great manager, he's worried about everybody," Martinez said. "He's worried about the guy on the bench who is not playing that day. He wants everybody to do well. That year, 1996, he became a leader on the field and in the clubhouse. He took control of the staff. We weren't expected to do much as a team. He didn't care about his hitting. If he struck out four times, he cared only about his pitcher. He wanted to call a great game. All he was concerned about was the wins and losses. He wasn't worried about his average or how many guys he threw out, it was all about winning, and he was happy."

Girardi became the player, the leader that Torre could lean on, and that kind of leadership rubbed off on the rest of the team. It was about "us" as a team, not "I."

"Another thing he brought along was his work ethic," Martinez said. "He's a hard-working guy, in the weight room all the time, he is probably the most fit guy on the team."

Girardi is still the fittest guy on his team at the age of 47.

"He was a great guy to learn from, too," Martinez explained. "I was kind of young, and he taught me maturity. I was struggling badly, wasn't sure if I was going to make it in New York or not, and he kept it in perspective for me, saying 'It's baseball.' I will never forget that."

That's all it is, baseball. Even though Girardi possesses that over-intense look all the time, even though he looks like his stomach is tied in knots during a game, and you can be sure it is, deep down he has a deeper understanding, "It's baseball."

Even for the Yankees, it's baseball.

If there is one play that represents Girardi's Yankees career from a highlight standpoint, it is the triple he lashed against Maddux in Game 6 of the 1996 World Series. To see him flying around the bases, practically running on air, is something Martinez said he will never forget.

"He was not known for his hitting, but that was probably the biggest hit that got this dynasty going," Martinez said. "Everybody talks about Jim Leyritz' home run off Mark Wohlers and [Andy] Pettitte's great pitching in Atlanta, but Joe's hit was crucial. It was a tie game at that time. That hit got us going, and I don't think that hit gets enough credit for getting this dynasty going. It took a load of pressure off us and gave us a ton of momentum. That hit right there almost closed the Braves out."

The Braves won 96 games that season, the Yankees won 92. Bobby Cox' team swept the Dodgers in the opening round of the playoffs and then had to fight through seven games to beat the Cardinals and get to the World Series.

This was the start of a beautiful baseball relationship.

After losing the first game against the Rangers in the ALDS, the Yankees won three straight close games and then got past the Orioles to set up the World Series matchup. Girardi hit only .238 in the first two series, but one of his five hits was a triple off David Wells in Game 2 against Baltimore in the ALCS, a sign of things to come. The Yankees lost that game, though. His next postseason triple proved to be a series-changer and a hit that kick-started the Yankees' dynasty.

Game 6 was scoreless going into the bottom of the third when Paul O'Neill led off the inning with a double off Maddux. The Yankees led the Series 3–2; they just needed one more offensive explosion to win their fourth straight game after the Braves had crushed the Yankees in the first two games of the Series, winning the opener at Yankee Stadium 12–1 and the second game 4–0.

This was a much different Yankees crowd back then. The Yankees had not won a World Series since 1978. They had not won a World Series game at home the entire Series, having lost those first two games in the Bronx. They had not won a World Series game at home since October 21, 1981, a 3–0 win over the Dodgers in Game 2 of a Series they would lose in six games. In Game 6 of that Series, they were crushed at Yankee Stadium, 9–2 by the Dodgers.

This was a Yankees crowd that was hungry, desperate, a crowd that had not known a championship in so many years, a crowd that wanted to believe.

This was a loud crowd, a crowd that would shake Yankee Stadium with cheers of thunder.

A groundout moved O'Neill to third, bringing Girardi, the No. 9 hitter to the plate with young Derek Jeter on deck. If Maddux could get Girardi out without giving up the run, the Braves might get out of this jam. But Girardi was up to the task and tripled to center field. He raced around the bases as Yankee Stadium exploded into a sea of noise with O'Neill dancing home, giving the Yankees a 1–0 lead.

The pressure was off. The Yankees, only one win away from World Series victory, had the lead, and the top of the order was coming up. Jeter followed with a single to left that scored Girardi and put the Yankees on top 2–0. Jeter stole second base. Wade

Boggs popped up for the second out of the inning, but Bernie Williams singled to center to score Jeter, and the Yankees led 3–0.

A new Yankees dynasty was about to be born.

Now it was just a question of getting 18 more outs, and you know that was the first thing that went through Girardi's mind as the catcher. The Yankees got it done. Jimmy Key went 5⅓ innings, with David Weathers and Graeme Lloyd getting through the sixth inning, and then young and spectacular Mariano Rivera arrived for two shutout innings followed by closer John Wetteland. Wetteland would win the World Series MVP as he got through the ninth, allowing one run but getting the three outs needed.

The Yankees had their 3–2 victory and their first World Series title in 18 years. Girardi's triple was the key hit.

Looking back on that day and that triple 15 years later, Girardi said soulfully, "It's the one moment in time that I wish I could go back to. Just because I don't remember it necessarily like everyone else remembered it because it happened so fast. I was locked into the game. And to hear Paul O'Neill say it was the loudest the Stadium has ever been, I don't remember that."

How could he remember? He was too locked in to doing his job. But what he does remember is steaming around the bases, saying with a smile, "It felt like I was running on air."

And all the hard work of a lifetime, all the times hitting with his dad, Jerry, it paid off that day because Girardi said it was "my biggest hit of the biggest game of my career."

Imagine connecting for the biggest hit of your career and never hearing the loudest crowd. Girardi was oblivious to what was going on around him at the time. It is amazing what the game of baseball can do to your senses. Girardi was so locked into the moment, so locked into the at-bat against a Hall of Fame pitcher, he never heard the cheers.

He really never took the time to enjoy the moment. It was about getting the job done, not basking in the moment of glory, it was about getting the outs needed to wrap up the game.

Martinez was not surprised to hear that Girardi did not hear the crowd that day. "He was so into the moment, and if he was thinking about anything at that point, he was thinking about outs to get," Martinez noted.

Always one step ahead. That's the Girardi way.

Girardi soon had the first of his three Yankees World Series rings.

You can be sure that when the Yankees get a lead now, Girardi is thinking, 'How are we going to get the outs needed to close this game?' There is no time to hear the cheers.

Girardi could always run well for a catcher, though. Perhaps it was the old football quarterback in him. That was a great year for Girardi all around. He hit a career-high .294 and stole a career-high 13 bases that season. That was the most for a catcher in the majors that season and established a Yankees record for stolen bases by a catcher in a season.

"He could always run for a catcher," said Yankees super-scout Gene "Stick" Michael, who had been the general manager before Watson and was instrumental in putting together the team that developed into a dynasty. "He was probably a 50–55 runner," Michael said, using the scouting terminology for grading a runner. That scale runs 20 to 80 and 55 is a high mark for a catcher. "And Joe always took care of himself," Michael added. "He was always in top shape. Even today he looks like he could play."

As a manager, Michael said that Girardi has a way about him to get his players to play hard. "He is consistent with his managing," Michael noted. "Nobody ever agrees with everybody on every move, but overall, I think he is very good. I don't think he is difficult to play for. He has intensity, but I don't think he is difficult to play for."

During his playing career there were so many special days with the Yankees. One of them came early in that first year on May 14, 1996, against Seattle when Dwight Gooden pitched a no-hitter at Yankee Stadium and Girardi was the catcher. Gooden has gone through so many troubled times since then, and Girardi felt for Gooden, telling reporters in March 2010 after Gooden had run into more trouble: "Your heart goes out to him. He was a great teammate. Doc and I will always be linked in a sense, played on championship teams and a no-hitter together."

In that game, Girardi batted second and went 1-for-3 with a run scored. This was a Yankees team that was just beginning to come into its own. Jeter was batting ninth that day. Alex Rodriguez was a young star for the Mariners and in the first inning drove the ball to deep center where Gerald Williams made a spectacular catch. To show how different those times were, the Yankees regularly sell out these days, but on that game in the Bronx the crowd was only 20,786.

Girardi had his work cut out for him that day as Gooden walked six and threw two wild pitches. Girardi was there to guide Doc home. It was an inspirational performance because Gooden had nearly been released. He entered that start with a 1–3 record and a 5.67 ERA.

The ninth inning was harrowing as Gooden surrendered a walk to Rodriguez, got Ken Griffey Jr. to ground out to first. Another walk to Edgar Martinez put runners on first and second. Gooden then uncorked a wild pitch to move the runners up. A base hit would have ended the no-hitter and tied the game. Gooden reached back for some magic from his Dr. K days and struck out Jay Buhner swinging and retired Paul Sorrento on a pop to Jeter to end the game as Girardi rushed to the mound to embrace Gooden.

That pitch was the 134th pitch of the night for Gooden. Gooden was carried off the field in triumph by his teammates. He finished the season 11–7 with a 5.01 ERA and was left off the postseason roster.

Reflecting back on that day years later, Gooden said, "To make it back and throw a no-hitter, that was an incredible blessing. No one in the world thought I could still do this, and it was the greatest feeling in the world. I owe so much to George Steinbrenner."

As for his own life, which has been tormented by alcohol and drug problems, Gooden believes he is finally on the right path, saying that once again a Steinbrenner had helped him, Hank Steinbrenner.

"Hank has really been great," Gooden said. "He's been a friend, always there in times of trouble. I enjoy my conversations with Hank. He's a lot like his father. He loves to win. He's been a friend, that's most important. I respect that, it means a lot to me.

"I've forgiven myself, that's the start of getting on the right road," Gooden added. "I had a hard time forgiving myself for all the shame, the guilt, not really being the father I know I could be, not really being the son I could be. Now I'm coming to grips with forgiving myself. I'm not a real religious person, but I realize that God forgave me, so who am I not to forgive myself? That has helped me turn the corner."

So what does Gooden see now when he looks in the mirror? He said, "I see peace. I see peace and joy. Just a year ago when I looked in the mirror, I saw a lot of hurt and pain. I am so blessed to be where I am now. Let me tell my story in a way I can touch others. That's what I want to do. If I don't take care of myself first, I won't get the opportunity to help others or help my kids. I have seven kids and two grandchildren. I love being with my kids."

Girardi also was the catcher for one of the most perfect days in Yankee Stadium history, a day you could not have planned any more perfectly.

In his final season with the Yankees on July 18, 1999, Girardi was behind the plate when David Cone threw his perfect game on Yogi Berra Day, of all days. That was a magical day from the start as Don Larsen, who pitched the only perfect game in World Series history in Game 5 over the Brooklyn Dodgers in the 1956 World Series with Yogi behind the plate in the 2–0 win, threw out the ceremonial first pitch to Yogi.

Of the two games, Gooden's no-hitter and Cone's perfect game, Girardi said the perfect game was more thrilling because of how rare those games are and there was simply no room for error. "You just couldn't have any type of mistake," Girardi said of that day when Cone's slider was on fire.

Cone put it in perspective, saying how all the Yankees' stars had aligned with the battery for the 1956 World Series perfect game in attendance. "You probably have a better chance of winning the lottery than this happening," Cone told reporters after the game.

Girardi said in 2011 that he always enjoyed the big days at Yankee Stadium and other ballparks, noting, "When I was a player on an opposing team, I always liked being around big events. Whether it was a Hall of Famer coming back, I always enjoyed it because it was the history of the game."

Girardi loves the history of the game. And on those days when you make history, it is even more special. Said Cone after his perfect game, "It makes you stop and think about the Yankees magic and the mystique of this ballpark."

Cone now calls that game his "signature moment."

The right-hander threw only 88 pitches that day, 68 for strikes and did not go to a three-ball count on a hitter on the scorching hot afternoon in the Bronx. Cone also had to sit through a 33-minute rain delay to reach perfection.

When the last out was made, a Cone slider that induced Montreal's Orlando Cabrera to pop to third baseman Scott Brosius in foul territory, Girardi raced out to greet Cone as the pitcher fell to his knees and put his hands over his head in jubilation. Cone fell into Girardi's arms with Girardi falling backward onto the Yankee Stadium grass, the two men hugging in triumph.

It is a lasting image of the joy and the unpredictability of the game. Every day something magical can happen in baseball. Cone is super-competitive but also is a player with a great sense of humor and a great sense of leadership. He was a leader in that clubhouse, just as Girardi was throughout his career.

In so many ways it was the perfect day in what was to be Girardi's final season as a Yankees player.

14.

BLEEDING CUBBIE BLUE

THE DREAM BEGAN to take shape in the third grade. Joe Girardi wrote a class paper—if you ever saw the 1983 film *A Christmas Story*, where all the kids in the class let out a groan as Miss Shields assigns a "theme"—you get the picture.

Instead of writing about wanting a Red Ryder BB gun, Girardi wrote about growing up to be a Chicago Cub. Amazingly, the local kid did just that. He became a Cub. Not once but twice.

As a kid, going to Cubs games was a huge treat for Girardi. His summer days were jam-packed with fun, playing baseball and Wiffle ball with his close friend, Todd Mervosh, challenging him to board games, eating peanut butter and jelly sandwiches, and dreaming he played for the Cubs.

"I would leave the house at 8:00 in the morning in the summers and go play with Todd until 5:00 o'clock at night, and we would play everything from Wiffle ball, to basketball to 100 by ones, to Clue, Risk," Girardi remembered. "When we played Wiffle ball, I was the Cubs, Todd was the Cardinals, and you had to hit accordingly, who was right-handed or left-handed. He lived five houses down. And at 5:00 o'clock my parents would yell for me to come home, and I'd go home. It was great."

This really was the all-American upbringing. And the Cubs were always his team.

"Glenn Beckert was one of my heroes," Girardi said. "We grew up watching him, Ron Santo, Jose Cardenal, and Don Kessinger. We grew up watching all of them. Ron Santo and Jose Cardenal were my two favorite players as a kid, and I got to know Santo really well when I became a Cub. He used to throw BP to me in the winter. We used to go out to dinner with him, Vicki [Santo's wife], Kim, and my in-laws. He lived nearby. Jose was my coach. I loved him."

In the Wiffle ball games, Girardi would run down the Cubs batting order just as so many other kids did throughout the country with their favorite players and favorite teams. Just imitating your favorite player's batting stance in a Wiffle ball game or a stickball game made them come alive. These were the video games of the time, and you got to be your heroes. Summer days would fly by, and the allegiance to your team would grow by the day.

You were not only watching your favorite players on television or listening on the radio, you became them in the games you played with your friends. It was the essence of being a young fan, and those memories and allegiances last forever. At its essence, that is the beauty of baseball.

On April 6, 1973, the Cubs beat the Expos 3–2 on Opening Day at Wrigley Field. Whitey Lockman was the Cubs manager. Gene Mauch managed the Expos. The Cubs would finish fifth that season. Girardi was eight years old. The lineup that day consisted of the likes of Jose Cardenal, batting second and playing right field, and Ron Santo, who was in his last season as a Cub, batted fifth, and picked up two hits. Tony LaRussa pinch ran for him in the ninth and scored the winning run as the Cubs scored twice in the inning to win. That turned out to be the last major league run

LaRussa would score. It was his last appearance in a major league game. LaRussa didn't know it at the time, but he had 33 years of major league managing in front of him and 5,097 regular season games, six pennants, and three World Series in his future.

Glenn Beckert batted sixth that day. In the summer of 2011, Beckert came to a Yankees-Rays game at Tropicana Field, and the moment Girardi saw him during batting practice, he dashed from the back of the batting cage, where he usually stands closely watching BP, and into the stands to welcome Beckert. The two men then walked onto the field and talked for 20 minutes. Girardi was as thrilled as if he were eight years old, meeting his baseball hero.

Baseball memories last forever.

"To see him around is great," Girardi said that day of Beckert, the inner-Cub in him aglow. "He lives in the St. Petersburg area. I love seeing him. The one guy that I don't see is Kessinger. I used see Santo all the time."

Ron Santo finally made the Hall of Fame in December of 2011, a reward that was long overdue for his career in baseball and his broadcasting career. Santo was elected one year and two days after he died. The former third baseman was a lovable Cub to the end. He was elected by the new Golden Era Committee, receiving 15 of 16 votes. Santo was a nine-time All-Star, an on-base percentage star before those numbers became popular with the Sabermetrics crowd, a gifted fielder who won five Gold Gloves, and, most importantly, won the hearts of so many fans because he played in an era when the team struggled. The fans loved their players as if they were family. Santo played for the Cubs for 14 seasons. Only three times did the Cubs finish as high as second place during those years, and those were the later years when there was divisional play.

None of that really mattered. The fans loved Santo and they loved their Cubs. This was pure baseball love.

And then when Santo went to the broadcast booth, a new generation of Cubs fans fell in love with him because they loved his passion for the Cubbies and how he rooted them on every day. This was much more than a game, and Santo became a part of every fan's family, being invited into their homes for the broadcast each day of the long season.

After he was elected, Vicki Santo told reporters in a conference call, "Such an honor for Ron, my initial emotion is, 'We dared to dream this.' He was always meant to be in the Hall of Fame. It was so important to Ron."

And to so many Cubs fans who have never seen their team win a World Series, now, at least, they have their hero in the Hall of Fame. Yes, Ron Santo was meant to be in the Hall of Fame.

For young Joe Girardi the really special summer days consisted of going to Wrigley Field with his dad and enjoying the day, taking in the atmosphere of that classic ballpark that takes you back in baseball time. So many ballparks these days have become sectioned off, where the luxury suite–fan has so many more privileges than the average fan. At Wrigley there is no distinction. Everyone is just a Cubs fan, and so it was for the Girardi family on special outings. While other ballparks in that time were cold, multi-use stadiums, Wrigley Field had a heart.

"The best part of the day was eating pizza at the park, I absolutely loved it," Girardi reminisced one day with Jack Curry on *The Joe Girardi Show* on YES.

This wasn't just any pizza, this was Ron Santo Pizza.

"I had so many great memories of those days," Girardi said. "Ron Santo and Jose Cardenal were my two favorite players. The reason Jose Cardenal was one of our favorite players is we actually thought he looked like my aunt. Now, I don't want to embarrass my Aunt Connie or Jose Cardenal. My aunt had this big Afro like Jose Cardenal, and we used to joke about it.

"When I got the chance to sit down with Jose when he was a coach with the Yankees, that was really a thrill for me," Girardi added.

Now that is family.

Girardi was busy at that time chasing some early baseball dreams, playing with the Sea Merchants. He was one of the best at running the Sea Merchant Mile. He also was eventually switched to catcher by his coach, Dave Rodgers, so he was trying to learn all facets of the game while watching the Cubs play and eating his Ron Santo Pizza.

Of his early success in the game, Girardi noted, "It was my determination and my passion for the game that helped me succeed. And the work ethic that I saw at home, how to persevere. You didn't let anything bother you. You didn't let anything get in your way—that really helped me. And I loved the strategy of the game."

Girardi was fascinated by baseball numbers from the start, telling the *Harvard Business Review* in 2010, "I love numbers. You can never give me too many numbers. I believe they tell a story. If you have a large enough sample. I have an industrial engineering degree—a degree in problem-solving, basically. But my whole family is math-oriented, and that's always been how I see things."

That puts the infamous Girardi binder into its proper perspective. The binder is an extension of his love for numbers, his math-oriented attention to detail.

When Girardi played travel baseball as a youngster, this was a much different time than the travel teams of today and the organized sports schedule that many child athletes follow from the time they join eight-and-under travel teams. "You didn't go to as many camps as kids now," Girardi explained. "I'd go to maybe one camp a year. I was lucky enough to go to the Purdue basketball camp."

He wasn't big enough for basketball or football, though. That's why baseball became his game.

This was a much different looking Joe Girardi, too. The Joe Girardi eating the Ron Santo Pizza at Wrigley Field had long hair for a while before going back to the crew cut that his father preferred.

Those Cubs were the lovable Cubbies. During that era the Cubs never saw the postseason. They played in the 1945 World Series and lost in seven games to the Tigers.

They haven't been back to the World Series since. The Cubs haven't won a World Series since 1908. That's one of the reasons Theo Epstein, the former Red Sox GM, left Boston for the Cubs. With the young Epstein as GM of the Red Sox, Boston got rid of the Curse of the Bambino by beating the Yankees in 2004, coming back from a 3–0 deficit, to win the American League pennant and then sweeping the Cardinals in the World Series. In 2007 Theo's Red Sox won a second World Series, beating the Rockies. If Theo someday wins a World Series with the Cubs, he will become a baseball legend.

Before winning the 2004 World Series, the Red Sox had not won a World Series since 1918, when they beat—you guessed it— the Cubs. Boston won with a lefty pitcher named Babe Ruth winning two of the games for them. Ruth could hit, too, having tied for the major league lead in home runs that year as a part-time hitter with 11, and saw five at-bats in that Series. His one hit was a triple that drove in two runs.

The next season the Red Sox had the foresight to make Ruth an everyday player, and the Bambino led the majors with 29 home runs. He also led the AL in RBIs with 114, 103 runs scored, a .456 on-base percentage, a .657 slugging percentage, 1.114 OPS, and 284 total bases.

George Herman Ruth was the most amazing player the game had ever seen, and he was only 24 years old. So, naturally, the Red Sox sold him to the Yankees on January 3, 1920, and thus was born the Curse of the Bambino.

The Cubs have their own curse, and it remains ever-present, the Curse of the Billy Goat. This curse only dates back to the 1945 World Series when Cubs fan and Billy Goat Tavern owner Billy Sianis brought his pet goat to the game and occupied two box seats, one for him and one for his goat. That was the fourth game of the World Series with the Cubs leading 2–1. The goat was decked out with a sweater that read: "We Got Detroit's Goat."

Some fans complained about the smell of the goat. Cubs owner P.K. Wrigley had Sianis and his goat escorted out of the ballpark, and Sianis promptly put a hex on the team. Legend has it he exclaimed, "The Cubs ain't gonna win no more!"

He was right. The Cubs haven't won since, and there have been some peculiar circumstances in their most painful losses. There was the black cat crossing in front of the dugout in 1969 against the Miracle Mets; there was first baseman Leon Durham having a ground ball dribble through his legs against the Padres in the 1984 playoffs; and there was fan Steve Bartman getting in the way on a foul ball in 2003 against the Marlins when the Cubs were five outs from finally returning to the World Series.

The curse lives on in so many ways. There are such Cubs fan websites as Goat Riders of the Apocalypse to keep it all so alive and so unreal.

This is the team that Joe Girardi was drafted by in the 1986 draft and played for from 1989 through 1992, hitting .262 with three home runs in 964 plate appearances.

During his first season in the minors, Girardi did not even have to leave home. He played for the Class A Peoria Chiefs. Girardi knows the importance of a first impression, and he made a good one on the Cubs. Over 68 games in Peoria, he batted .309 over 230 at-bats. Young teammate Mark Grace was the big hitter on the ballclub, smacking 15 home runs to Girardi's three and batting an eye-popping .342, but Girardi established himself quickly as a ballplayer.

Girardi recalled those days in an interview with ESPN's Andrew Marchand in June 2011. "When I was drafted by the Cubs, Pete Vonachen, the owner of the Peoria Suns, asked for me to play in my hometown. They sent me right to the Midwest League. We had a lot of commuter trips. My dad, every day before he went to work, had a sandwich ready for me. He went to every game we were at home. He just made life easy for me."

In 2011 the Cubs honored Vonachen in a game against the Cardinals at Wrigley Field. Vonachen purchased the Peoria Suns three years before Girardi was drafted. He changed their name to the Chiefs, and the club went on to set Midwest League attendance records with the likes of Girardi, Grace, and Greg Maddux playing at Meinen Field, which was renamed Pete Vonachen Stadium in 1992. Cubs fans are loyal fans in the majors and the minors.

Girardi would steadily move up the ladder.

He played at Winston-Salem in 1987 and hit .280 over 99 games and 364 at-bats. His leadership with the young pitchers was invaluable. The next season he moved onto Double A Pittsfield, where Girardi batted .272 over 104 games. That was the season he met a young pitcher, a man with whom he would be friends for life, Mike Harkey. Harkey was 21; Girardi was 23. They became fast friends. The imposing Harkey burst onto the scene with a 9–2 record and a 1.37 ERA.

"We're complete opposites, but we immediately bonded," Girardi said 23 years later. Harkey is still with Girardi to this day as Yankees bullpen coach and remains one of his closest friends and a sounding board for Girardi in so many ways. Harkey is always quick to kid with Girardi and is not afraid to get on his manager in a fun-loving way. They essentially are still two young teammates in Double A.

In 1989 Girardi made it all the way to the majors with the Cubs, his baseball dream coming true as he was the Cubs Opening Day catcher. Fleer produced a "prospects" card for the Cubs that season that featured two Cubs prospects, a smiling, square-jawed Girardi and outfielder Rolando Roomes. Roomes would play three seasons, a total of 170 games in the majors but only 17 with the Cubs. Girardi would play 15 seasons in the majors.

That season Girardi became the first rookie catcher to start a season opener for the Cubs since Randy Hundley in 1966 and was selected to *Baseball Digest*'s All-Rookie team. The major league minimum at the time was $68,000, and Girardi was in baseball heaven, playing for his beloved Cubs even though the challenge was difficult.

Girardi continued to put in the hard work and also played in the Winter League for Aguilas del Zulia in the Venezuelan Winter League in 1989.

He still had some minor league time to put in and played 32 games at Triple A Iowa that season, batting .245, three points below the .248 average he put up for the Cubs over 59 games. The following year, 1990, Girardi played the entire season in the majors with the Cubs. His eight stolen bases were the most by a Cubs catcher since Gabby Hartnett stole 10 bases in 1924. Girardi was solid behind the plate, throwing out 33 percent of the base runners who tried to steal on him (38-of-114), and hit a solid .270.

Girardi was tough and did not suffer many serious injuries, but a sore lower back kept him sidelined for nearly four months in 1991. Naturally, his first game back he was involved in a collision at home plate with Philadelphia's John Kruk, as Girardi suffered a broken nose. Girardi was always there to block the plate.

After the 1992 season, Girardi went to the Rockies in the expansion draft. He spent the next three seasons there before being traded out of the National League and to the Yankees, where he had so much success over four seasons.

With the emergence of the young Jorge Posada as catcher for the Yankees, it was time for Girardi to move on again, and on December 15, 1999, he signed as a free agent back with his beloved Cubs, back to the Curse of the Billy Goat. You can go home again in baseball.

That first season back, the 35-year-old Girardi played in 106 games, batted .278, knocked in 40 runs, and hit six home runs, two below his career high. He was a productive veteran, but more importantly, he was a leader on that team. Those Cubs needed all the leadership they could get that season, as they were 65–97. This was a long way from the success of the Yankees, who would go on to beat the Mets in the 2000 World Series. The Yankees were winning their third World Series in four years under Joe Torre. Girardi was trying to hold on to his career with a struggling Cubs team in Chicago.

But, for Girardi, it was time to be back in the Midwest, and he spent the next three seasons with the Cubs. This was a life experience. This was about coming home, not just some numbers on a page.

There were highlights, of course. When he rejoined the Cubs in 2000, he earned his first and only trip to an All-Star Game that July in Atlanta. He was added to the team as a replacement for Mike Piazza. Piazza had to come off the team because Roger Clemens hit him in the head with a pitch on July 8. At that point the calls went out, and Girardi, who was hitting .302, gladly accepted. He did not play in the 6–3 AL victory, the only position player not to get in the game, but he loved his experience of being an All-Star for the one and only time in his career. His former teammate, Derek Jeter, was named MVP of the game. The Yankees ruled baseball in so many ways at the time.

Girardi's first Cubs homer the second time around came against Jose Lima on May 2, 2000, in the fifth inning with one on in an 11–1 win over the Astros at Wrigley Field.

That was Girardi's first Cubs home run since May 8, 1992, at Wrigley. This blast came in the second inning of a 10–7 loss off Jose Rijo. Future Yankees teammate Paul O'Neill was in right field for the Reds that day and went 3-for-6 to raise his batting average to .351. Girardi's teammate was Greg Maddux, who went 20–11 that season. Four years later in the World Series, Girardi would hit his big triple off Maddux. Ryne Sandberg and Andre Dawson, two future Hall of Famers, were in the lineup that day for the Cubs, as was Sammy Sosa.

The 1992 Cubs finished 78–84 in fourth place, 18 games back of Barry Bonds' Pirates. The 2000 Cubs finished dead last in the Central Division at 65–97, 30 games back of the Cardinals.

This was a long way from the success of the Yankees.

The next season on May 27, 2001, Girardi collected his 1,000th major league hit off the Brewers' Jimmy Haynes, and this was a big one, a game-winning two-run double in a 4–1 victory. Girardi's hit snapped a 1–1 tie as the Cubs scored four times in that inning to win.

Those were heady days for the Cubs, who were in first place on their way to a 51–35 mark and a .593 winning percentage the first half of the season. The Cubs faded in the second half, though, going 37–39 on their way to a third-place finish behind the Astros.

Girardi always stood his ground as a ballplayer, and one day he even dared to tell Sosa to turn down the volume on his boom box, but Girardi insists that it was simply a case of his thinking Sosa had gone to the cage to hit so that is why he turned it down. He explained that, at the age of 37, he wasn't a big fan of loud music at 9:00 AM.

"I like music in the clubhouse, though," he would say years later. "It's uplifting."

Girardi was there to help lift the Cubs in good days and in bad. He was named cocaptain in 2001 and 2002. In his final season in Chicago, 2002, the Cubs went backward again, posting a 67–95 mark and finishing fifth, 30 games behind the division-winning Cardinals.

One of the worst days of his career was June 22, 2002, at Wrigley Field. Before the game it was learned that St. Louis pitcher Darryl Kile passed away in his hotel room in Chicago, and Girardi had to come out to announce to the sellout crowd that the game had been postponed. Girardi was the starting catcher that day and was going out to warm up the Cubs' starter when he noticed that the Cardinals bench was empty. He soon was informed of the terrible news, and his heart sank.

Kile and Girardi were on the 2000 NL All-Star team. Kile and his wife were the parents of three young children. Cubs president Andy MacPhail asked Girardi to tell the crowd that the game had been postponed. Girardi was given the public address microphone to make the announcement and told the fans, "Thanks for your patience. I regret to inform you that because of a tragedy in the Cardinals' family, today's game has been canceled."

Making the announcement, Girardi explained years later, "was the hardest thing I ever had to do in the game of baseball."

After making that announcement, a fan screamed: "What happened?" Girardi then said into the microphone, "Please be respectful, when you find out eventually what has happened, I ask that you say a prayer for the St. Louis Cardinals family."

In 2006 Girardi recalled that terrible day as he told NJ.com, "You think about, 'How do you call his wife? How does the wife tell her kids?' Because I had a wife and kids, I was thinking, 'How does someone call and do that.' A very sad day."

Joe Girardi has known more than his share of sad days with his mother dying at such a young age and his father's long and difficult battle with Alzheimer's.

Teammates said at the time that Girardi was the perfect choice by MacPhail to make the announcement because he was so respected by everyone on both teams. Essentially, at that point in his career, Girardi was a coach on the field.

Girardi would have one more season in the majors. He signed with the Cardinals at the age of 38. He was able to stay in the Midwest and be near his dad. In his final year in the majors, Girardi appeared in only 16 games, had 23 at-bats, and three hits. But he was reunited with Tino Martinez and got to see a young Albert Pujols destroy opposing pitching. Pujols blasted 43 home runs that season, lashed 51 doubles, and drove in 124 runs.

This was a new era in baseball, and Pujols' Cardinals would win two World Series, in 2006 and 2011. The Cardinals also made it to the 2004 World Series, where they were swept by Epstein's Red Sox. From 2004 to 2011, the Cardinals' archrivals, the Cubs, did not win a single postseason game. Only twice did the Cubs even make it to October. In 2007 and 2008 the Cubs were swept 3–0 in the NLDS, the first time by the Diamondbacks, the second time by the Dodgers.

The Curse of the Billy Goat lives.

The 2003 season in St. Louis was the end of the playing line for Girardi. In his last at-bat, Girardi went out with a base hit, a ninth-inning single off Arizona's Edgar Gonzalez in Arizona in a 9–5 win. That hit gave him 1,100 career hits. It was a good way to leave. His manager that day was Tony LaRussa, who had been the pinch runner for Ron Santo in that Cubs Opening Day victory 30 years earlier. The game tells you when it is time to go as a player.

It was time for Girardi to move on to another phase of his career. There was still so much to do in his baseball career. Two years later he would make his coaching debut with the Yankees, serving as bench coach and catching instructor for Joe Torre. A year after that he made his managing debut with the Marlins. Two years later he became the Yankees manager. The game moves on.

Someday, Girardi could wind up back in the Midwest, maybe even as the manager of his beloved Cubs.

Those close to him would not be surprised if that happened, if the timing were right. When the Cubs had a managerial opening and hired Mike Quade, as Girardi's first Yankees contract was expiring, the timing was all wrong for Girardi. It was near the end of the 2010 season. He was coming off the 2009 World Series championship with the Yankees. He had already changed his number to 28. Girardi was established as a manager with the Yankees, and his family had put down roots in the New York area. It was no time to move.

"Managing the Cubs probably is Joe's dream job, but right now the timing isn't right," Girardi's friend Bob Manning told the *Chicago Tribune* in late August 2010 when the Yankees were in Chicago to play a series against the White Sox. "Maybe after winning another World Series or two with the Yankees, he'll want to take on that challenge. But in Joe's mind it's all about winning, and he knows the Yankees are committed to that."

The timing was not right to uproot his family out of the New York suburbs with the kids in school and heavily involved in extracurricular activities. For Girardi, family always comes first, but, sure, there could come a time when Girardi manages the Cubs, because the Cubs will always be family to him.

At the time when those rumors swirled, Girardi made it clear that it was the Yankees family that he was devoted to, telling the New York media, "I have a responsibility to the organization and to the guys in that clubhouse," he said of his Yankees players. "That's where my focus is. I'm very happy here. This organization has been great to me."

Girardi had let Brian Cashman know in early August that he wanted to stay with the Yankees. The Cubs situation never really was a factor.

The Yankees soon took care of Girardi after the 2010 season. Cashman did not want Girardi to get away. Cashman is all about stability for the Yankees, and Girardi is at the center of that plan. On October 29, the Yankees announced that they re-signed Girardi to a three-year contract through the 2013 season, a deal that pays Girardi $3 million a season, making him one of the highest-paid managers in the game. At the time the pact was announced, the Yankees made sure to point out that even with missing the post-season in 2008, the Yankees had gone a major league best 287–199 (a .591 winning percentage) since 2008 under Girardi.

That's winning. That is what Joe Girardi is all about.

Add the Yankees 2011 regular season record (97–65) to the mix, and it's even better. Overall, under Girardi, the Yankees are 384–264, a .593 winning percentage with one World Series championship and three trips to the postseason in four years.

For Girardi it is all about winning, and with Theo Epstein hiring Dale Sveum to manage the Cubs in November 2011, any thoughts and dreams of someday managing the Cubbies will have to wait for quite some time. That's fine.

As for that 103-year championship drought for the Cubs, and that Billy Goat Curse, Sveum, the Brewers' former hitting coach and third-base coach for the Red Sox when Epstein was in Boston, told reporters on the day he was hired: "The past is the past no matter where you are. It really doesn't matter what happened in the past."

Those are the truest of baseball words, but there is no past like the Cubs' past.

15.

WINDS OF CHANGE

FIFTEEN YEARS OF major league baseball were hard work for Joe Girardi, make no mistake about that. As a player, Girardi said, the game was never really fun for him.

"You have fun, but I don't think you ever take the time to enjoy it," Girardi explained. "Because it's every day; it would be a much different sport if you played it once a week and took the time to savor it. But if you do that in baseball, you can get slapped in the face the next day. It's not like you can sit down and really enjoy it. You can enjoy it when the season is over and you can sit back and reflect on everything."

Girardi is so right about that. There is little time to take in the accolades in baseball. If you slip up, someone is waiting to shut you down the next pitch, the next at-bat, the next game, or the next season. Baseball is relentless.

Fun is playing with your kids or joking around with the coaches or players. "We have a lot of fun," Girardi said of his coaching staff. "I love the game and I love to have fun. But as a player it was just different. It's different when you are playing the game every day. You have to be prepared every day."

Then he added a most revealing comment: "It's like managing."

You have to be prepared every pitch, every game, every day. Managing is relentless.

Don Baylor was Girardi's manager with the Rockies and during his second go-round with the Cubs. No one knows him better in the game. Don Zimmer was one of Baylor's coaches and was Girardi's first manager when he came up to the majors with the Cubs in 1989.

Girardi was chosen in the expansion draft as the 19th pick by the Rockies in 1992. It was time to leave the Cubs, but in so many ways Girardi was home with the Rockies, and that became an incredible experience.

There were different expectations in Colorado because this was an expansion team. In a sense, it was a brand new baseball party, the GM was Bob Gebhard, and the Rockies were drawing Mile High crowds. It wasn't the Broncos, but it was a spectacle because pitching in Denver created a different kind of game, and Girardi was caught right in the middle of it.

Girardi was brought to Colorado for a specific reason, and it wasn't to have fun.

It was to be a coach on the field, even though Girardi was still a young player at the age of 28. Baylor wanted Girardi to take care of the pitchers and show them the major league way and not let their confidence disappear into thin air. None of that was easy in the rarified air of Denver, playing at Mile High Stadium, where that first season the Rockies pitching staff posted an ERA of 5.41. Mile High was a nightmare, but on the road, the Rockies pitching staff, guided by Girardi, put up a respectable—considering the expansion circumstances—4.97 ERA. The 1969 expansion San Diego Padres' ERA was 4.24, and in 1998 the expansion Tampa Bay Devil Rays posted a 4.35 ERA, so considering all the circumstances, the Rockies were in the ERA ballpark.

The young catcher on the team, backing up Girardi, was another future major league manager, Eric Wedge. The Rockies and Gebhard had a plan. They knew the pitching would be a challenge, so they stocked the team with intelligent catchers. There was Girardi, Wedge, and Jayhawk Owens, who was to become a successful minor league manager. In addition, they had Brad Ausmus, one of the headier players in the game, a graduate of Dartmouth College, who would play 18 seasons in the majors and is now in the front office of the perpetually rebuilding San Diego Padres. Ausmus was taken from the Yankees with the 54th pick in the expansion draft.

Ausmus was traded by the Rockies in July of 1993 to the Padres. Owens managed to play four seasons with the Rockies. Wedge played only 39 major league games, nine with the Rockies, and the other 30 with the Red Sox over parts of three seasons.

The Rockies were a fun team. They were 67–95 that inaugural season, but that was good enough to escape the NL West cellar— plus they won 31 of their final 52 games. The Padres were in one of their cutting-salary modes and finished last in the division with a 61–101 mark, embarrassed to trail an expansion team.

This was before the Central Division was conceived; the National League consisted of an East and a West. The Rockies' big hitter was Andres Galarraga, who led the National League in hitting with a .370 average. One of Joe's close friends on the team, Dante Bichette, also had a good year, batting .310, and became one of the "Blake Street Bombers" for the Rockies. Eighteen years later, the Yankees would draft Dante Bichette Jr., and the club is hoping that he is on the fast track to success.

Baylor knew exactly what he wanted from Girardi. "With Joe, I wanted him to take care of our pitching staff," he explained. That was a job in itself, but there was an unexpected bonus to what

Girardi produced as he batted .290. "He got a lot of key hits," Baylor said of Girardi's three years in Colorado. "He didn't put his offense first. He put his pitchers first to get them through. Some of the staffs we had, we had some fragile guys because they didn't have the humidor."

The room-sized humidor, which would cut home runs dramatically, came into play much later in Colorado. By keeping the baseballs in a humidor, it kept them from being hit out of the ballpark so easily. In 1993 there was no humidor, so balls flew all over the ballpark. Armando Reynoso was the ace of that first Rockies staff, compiling a 12–11 record and a remarkable 4.00 ERA, considering the circumstances. Reynoso even threw four complete games. The Rockies knew what they were doing, taking Reynoso out of the well-stocked Braves organization. The right-hander was a soft-tosser who would eventually need elbow surgery, but that season he saved the Rockies from losing 100 games.

Girardi had a simple plan whenever he would see a pitcher losing focus, and it meant a trip to the mound where he would remind his pitcher to change his rhythm a bit, simplify the game. He said every pitcher has one pitch that can get him back on track, and it is the catcher's job to find that pitch as soon as possible and make the most of that information.

"It's all about finding that one pitch," Girardi explained.

Huge crowds came to the games, and it took only 17 home games for the Rockies to hit the 1 million mark in attendance. It was a baseball happening. There was plenty of action at a game because of the poor pitching and the great hitting conditions.

The first two years the Rockies played at Mile High. In their third season they moved into their beautiful new downtown home, Coors Field, and the Rockies responded with a 77–67 record and, amazingly, by winning the wild-card. The Rockies went from an expansion team to a playoff team, seemingly overnight. Good times.

They called it "Baseball with Altitude." The catchy name for all the big hitters, the Blake Street Bombers, came about because Coors Field is located on the corner of 20th and Blake. The earliest an expansion team had ever made it to the playoffs, prior to the Rockies' success, was eight years.

That success came because the Rockies had the wisdom to sign Andres Galarraga as a free agent before they picked anyone in the 1992 expansion draft. They already had a hitting foundation. They could fill in the needed pieces. Girardi was a huge piece. Girardi caught 122 games that 1995 season. The Rockies' road ERA was the second best in the NL at 3.71. The Rockies had quickly come of age.

They finished only one game back of the Dodgers in second place in the NL West, essentially going from expansion team to a near division winner overnight. A lot of that was the leadership Girardi brought to the Rockies. The move to the Rockies really accelerated Girardi's leadership qualities because so much was expected of him with an expansion staff, and he delivered by helping to get those pitchers to the playoffs in just three seasons.

It was a formative time in Girardi's career, and in 2008, when he took over as manager of the Yankees, he told longtime baseball writer Gerry Fraley, "Without Colorado, I'm probably not sitting here. I've been very fortunate everywhere I played, but Colorado was a special experience."

The Rockies gave him the opportunity to excel and then traded him to the Yankees. The home opener opened his eyes, too, that first year as 80,227 fans poured into Mile High Stadium, a day that Girardi caught Bryn Smith in an 11–4 victory.

Baylor knew what he had in Girardi, a catcher who could guide a questionable pitching staff.

"Guys had 5.00 ERAs and high 4.00s, and you have to try to talk them through that," Baylor explained. "Joe really worked on the mental part of the game. I gave him that responsibility to get these pitchers through certain innings, certain situations. He was a kind of manager on the field with the pitchers, and he really enjoyed doing that. That helped him get ready to manage."

In a way, that is how Girardi had fun on the field as a player. By being a manager. That was his challenge, and he accepted it. Trying to guide others is what makes the game special to him. It is what he was born to do.

Harkey, who is a coach with the Yankees, was a teammate with Girardi in Colorado in 1994 and with the Cubs, said, "Joe was the leader. He was the most prepared guy I'd ever been around."

It's always about preparation for Girardi—that is a key to success. One other thing, Harkey said, when you were around Joe Girardi, "You learned."

That's the way it was with Girardi. And that is just the way Baylor knew it would be with Girardi behind the plate, that's why the Rockies brought him to Denver. With all the pieces fitting so well into place, the Rockies kept drawing huge crowds. Blake Street Bomber Vinny Castilla once noted of the crowds, "Whether it was raining or snowing or whatever, it was a packed house every day."

The Rockies eventually put together a sellout streak of 203 consecutive games.

Baylor is one of baseball's great treasures. He won Manager of the Year honors in 1995. He has been everywhere and has done everything, playing 19 seasons in the majors and helping take five different teams to the postseason. Much like Girardi, he was always like having an extra coach on the field when he was a player. He was one of those players who became the final piece to a team's puzzle, one of those players everyone else in the locker room looked up to. And, to this day, he is still that kind of person, and no matter where he goes, success follows him to the ballpark. He remains one of the best hitting coaches in the game. He remains a leader.

His Rockies had their troubles on the road because they were built for success at home. "We'd come home," he told MLB.com years later, "and all of a sudden we would be wearing that 'S' on our chest again."

The Rockies were Supermen once more at Coors Field, and Bichette was one of the players wearing that red cape in 1995. That season he led the National League in home runs (40), hits (197), RBIs (128), slugging percentage (.620), and total bases (359). It was "grip it and rip it" for Bichette.

The Rockies had the misfortune to match up against the Braves and lost in the first round in four games, but led in every game at one point. The Rockies just couldn't hold on for final victory, and the Braves won the World Series that season.

"It was the most fun I ever had in baseball," Baylor said of the run. Baylor is never hesitant to tell the truth. When he is told that Girardi said that he never really had fun as a player, Baylor smiled broadly and said, "He enjoyed playing, don't let him BS you. It was kind of tough for him because he had to work at everything. You don't get through major league baseball and have the success that he had after he left here going to New York [without having to work at it]. Guys loved throwing to him."

Yes, Baylor knew Girardi had to work overtime to overcome his offensive struggles, and he knows how hard he had to work to become the excellent defensive catcher that he became, but he also knows that Girardi had fun. And when Girardi left the Rockies and went to New York, he really had fun because that team won. Fun is winning for Joe Girardi.

"Going there to New York," Baylor said, "that place was really the stage for him. Certain guys can play in different places, but everybody cannot play in New York and be successful."

Girardi's triple in the 1996 World Series was his ultimate shining moment in New York, and Zimmer, who was the bench coach in Colorado as well as with Joe Torre in New York, put that play and Girardi in perfect perspective, saying, "He hit that ball in right-center field over their heads. I'm telling you, I thought I hit it, I was so happy for him. The one thing I've always said about Joe Girardi is that he is a winner, and that day he got a huge winning hit."

That was a fun day, even though as Girardi noted he never took the time to hear the crowd, he was so locked into the moment.

Baylor wasn't afraid to have a little fun with Girardi, either, as a manager. Here is what he did to his catcher one day in the heat of battle on the road in one of the most hostile environments in baseball, Veterans Stadium in Philadelphia.

"The scoreboard always put up where guys had gone to college, academic All-American, and Joe was one of those academic All-America guys," Baylor explained. "We were in Philadelphia one day, and there was bases loaded, and Darren Daulton was hitting. I went out to the mound, and Joe asked, 'Hey, Skip, what do you think we should do?'

"I said, 'Well, you're a four-year academic All-American,' and I walked away."

Baylor let it ride. He wanted his catcher to take complete control, and Girardi did just that.

"We got out of the situation," Baylor recalled. "We laughed about that later. He was good to have, because Zimmer had had him before in Chicago, and the three of us always interacted all the time. So it was a good flow for him."

Baylor and Zimmer were great for Girardi in so many ways. They were great for his career, great to learn from for future managerial reference points, and just great to be around as a player. In some ways Girardi had more fun in Colorado than anywhere else. He even had his own TV show in Colorado. That all came to an end, though, when Girardi was traded to the Yankees, a trade he quickly welcomed at the time.

Girardi earned his money with the Rockies and was the union rep for the team, and these were unstable times in baseball. The game did not have the labor success that it enjoys today. It was much more turbulent, much more like the NBA is today. The baseball players and owners had not yet figured out how to share the massive wealth the game could provide to both sides. Girardi played a prominent role with the Major League Players Association to try to make it better for both sides. When Girardi was traded after the 1995 season, there was talk his role in the Players Association played a role in the decision to get rid of a catcher who was a leader on and off the field for a team that just made a tremendous run. However, the Rockies maintained they were under the financial gun to pare down salary because they had just re-signed shortstop Walt Weiss and were going after free agent second baseman Craig Biggio, who was a free agent at the time.

Winning is never cheap. Teams learn that every year, and that is why the Yankees are such a great place to play and manage. The Yankees can afford to compete and keep their star players or sign new stars, whatever is needed at the time.

Biggio signed back with the Astros on December 14, 1995. Girardi was traded to the Yankees for pitcher Mike DeJean on November 20, 1995. DeJean was still in the minors at the time, so the Rockies were able to save some cash. In 1995 Girardi made $1.85 million.

In explaining the deal, Gebhard told Fraley, "I did not want to lose Joe, and Don did not want to lose Joe. He was vital to our success. But it was a dollars-and-cents decision."

Often the game is ruled by dollars and cents and not common sense. Girardi has always said about that deal and his baseball life, "I believe things happen for a reason."

He did not look back. Within a week of the trade, his answering machine featured Frank Sinatra's "New York, New York," explained a 1996 article on Girardi for *Yankees Magazine*. Start spreading the news. The Yankees were about to go on a championship run for the ages with Girardi behind the plate. Girardi has a great sense of where he is at every moment in his life and looks at everything as an opportunity. When Girardi left Denver, he had his eyes on the future but also respected the fact that the Rockies and life in Colorado were a blessing to him.

"We've definitely turned the page," he told *Yankees Magazine*, referring to himself and his wife, Kim. Everything in Girardi's life revolves around family. It is not just how a situation impacts him, but how it impacts the family—which is why he often answers personal questions with "we" not "I."

"It's time to move on for us," Girardi said. "We understand things like this are going to happen in baseball, and we look at it as a great opportunity. Going to New York, it's a great city. I look at where I've had a chance to play for the Chicago Cubs, tradition; Denver, expansion; and then the Yankees, probably the greatest tradition of all. I've been pretty lucky.

"I never expected to play this long," Girardi said at the time of the trade. "The opportunity that I've had to travel and live the life of an athlete, it's just been really rewarding. God's blessed us in a lot of ways, and we're very thankful for that."

As a manager, Girardi knows he is continuing to be blessed to work for the Yankees, and he is trying his best to loosen up, as well. Every spring training he has a day where the team leaves the Yankees training complex at George M. Steinbrenner Field and heads off to an afternoon of fun and games, which becomes a bonding experience. Loosening the reins a bit is always a good idea in the marathon that is a baseball season.

Baseball should be fun, at times.

There was even the situation late in the 2011 season where Girardi let Jorge Posada have some fun on the field. The season for

Posada was difficult in so many ways. He had his issues with Girardi and GM Brian Cashman, even getting so upset one day in May with how he was being used, when he was dropped to ninth in the order, that he pulled himself out of the lineup against the Red Sox to try to get his head straight.

Eventually, Posada did just that. He got his head straight. He got back to being the player the Yankees could count on and was an offensive force in the five-game series with the Tigers, batting .429 in the ALDS, a fitting end to his stellar career, as he retired after the 2011 postseason.

The toll of catching wears out a player, and Russell Martin, who replaced Posada in the starting lineup, was spent by the time the postseason rolled around, batting only .176 against the Tigers with no RBIs in 21 plate appearances. It's not easy being a catcher in the postseason.

From his first day as a Yankee to the 2011 season, Posada came so far as a player. He was selected in the 24th round of the 1990 draft. He shifted positions from second base to catcher to make it as a Yankee and became one of the greatest Yankees ever, part of the Core Four of Posada, Derek Jeter, Mariano Rivera, and Andy Pettitte who came up through the Yankees system and carried the Yankees to championships. It's about the rings in New York, and Posada and the Core Four have their rings.

During the regular season in 2011, Posada hit only .235 as a designated hitter (81-for-344). Most of his hits, though, were big hits. Making the adjustment from catcher to DH was extremely difficult for Posada. DH is a role where you have to find yourself and have to find something to do with all the time you suddenly have at a game, because all you are doing is hitting. You never get on the field. It is hard for position players to make the switch, but it is incredibly hard for catchers, who are involved in every pitch, to make the switch.

Some of the best DHs are players who really don't enjoy the defensive end of the game. Ex-Yankee and current Rockie Jason Giambi is the perfect example of a player who is made to DH. He never really enjoys playing first base, does not like to make that throw to second, so being a DH takes pressure off Giambi, and he was perfect for that role with the Yankees. To his credit, he has found a way to survive in the National League, where there is no DH. Giambi is a fearsome pinch-hitter for the Rockies and has always been considered a great teammate.

Giambi, going into his 18th season, welcomes young players to the team, is extremely generous with his money in picking up dinner tabs for teammates, and is always fun to be around. He has the mindset of a DH, free and easy. It is ironic, too, that Giambi, when he is on deck, never takes a swing. He does all his swinging in the cage or at the plate. As he stands on deck he works on timing the pitcher or just getting loose, but he never takes a swing.

Posada is the complete opposite, incredibly intense while the game is going on. That is how he got to be the player he became, ranking seventh on the Yankees' all-time list with 379 doubles and 963 walks. He is eighth in home runs with 275 and 11th in RBIs, collecting 1,065 in pinstripes.

Here is the best number, though. Posada's 246 home runs as a catcher ranks second all-time on the Yankees behind the one and only Yogi Berra (306). When it comes to Yankees catchers, Posada is in the top three when it comes to games caught with 1,574. Bill Dickey is first on the list with 1,708 games, and Berra is No. 2 with 1,695 games. That is quite a list.

Posada talked about the difficulty of moving to DH in spring training. "It's just a question of getting ready for your at-bats," he explained. "You really have to be loose, ride the bike, stretch, and get your eyes used to the sun or the lights."

Turns out it the mental adjustment to DH was just as difficult to make as those physical adjustments. In spring training Posada said he felt like he could continue to play for a couple more years. "I feel like I can still do it."

He said he would even consider leaving the Yankees to continue his career. A line was drawn in the sand. It was not going to be a smooth transition year for Posada, and Girardi was right in the middle of it. Going from full-time catcher to DH was extremely tough on Posada, especially since he struggled mightily hitting from the right side in 2011, where he batted only .092 with a .169 on-base percentage.

"It's been a struggle for him," Girardi admitted when he was forced to drop him in the lineup. "You just keep playing it out and hope that guys turn it around. I have a ton of respect for 'Georgie' over his career and the success that he has had. No one wants to be bumped down in the order, but with what Georgie has meant to this franchise and the success that he has had, it is a little more difficult. We need him to be productive as our DH. My hope is that he gets going."

Girardi genuinely felt for Posada.

As Posada dropped lower and lower in the lineup during the season, and his average dropped into the .100s in May, Posada said, "The only way I'm going to move up is to start producing. I'm still in there. I'm hitting ninth, but I've put myself in this spot. It's not like I want to hit ninth, it's not like I want to hit one-something. I've put myself in this spot and I need to get out of it."

Girardi recognized all this and in a game late in the year allowed Posada to have some fun. As the Yankees were trouncing the A's one late August day at Yankee Stadium, 22–9, Posada began pestering Girardi about playing second base, the position he originally came into the organization playing.

Posada made a deal with the skipper and the player he replaced as Yankees catcher. If the Yankees managed to score 18 runs, Posada could grab an infielder's glove and go play second base. Curtis Granderson's grand slam in the bottom of the eighth allowed Posada to do just that. And when Posada made his major league debut at second base in the top of the ninth, the Yankee Stadium crowd of 46,369 gave him an ovation. The Yankees fans have always admired Posada for his grit, determination, and ability to get a big hit, and this was a day to relax and enjoy as Russell Martin had one of his best days as a Yankee, going 5-for-5 with two home runs and six RBIs.

After the game, a smiling Girardi explained that Posada had been badgering him to make the move to put Posada at second base. Hitting coach Kevin Long, who might be the King of Badgering, was also nagging Girardi to make the move, so Girardi obliged.

Girardi let down his guard a bit and offered these words, "I think with everything Jorge has done for this organization, the numbers that he has put up, and the year that he has had through this year, it was just hard to say no."

Posada even got to field a ground ball for the last out of the game. He caught the grounder cleanly but delivered a hard, one-bounce throw that Nick Swisher had to scoop at first base.

It was the thought that counted, though, and Posada laughed about the play, saying, "I knew that last out was coming to me, it was a long time since I fielded a ground ball in the middle of the infield. Now you see why they moved me behind the plate. Got a good glove, no throw."

Posada then smiled. It was good to see him smile after such a trying season. When things were at their lowest during the year, Posada talked about how he hoped to salvage the season. "I just have to be prepared," he said. "From now on I have to look at the lineup card and be ready to play. I haven't given up."

His playing time had been cut, and he found out that morning he was in the lineup and made the most of the opportunity. That was the way it was going to be.

Posada did not give up, but in July things got even worse as Posada did not hit one home run and had but three RBIs. He finally broke out on August 13 at Yankee Stadium, hitting a grand slam off Tampa Bay's Brandon Gomes. He had three hits on the day and twice as many RBIs (six) as he had for the entire month of July. A weight had been lifted off his shoulders.

"I was happy," Posada said. "This is special. I got the opportunity today to play. It's tough to sit around. It's not easy to be sitting here with everyone else playing, it's tough."

The grand slam was the 10th of Posada's career, and it jumped him ahead of both Mickey Mantle and Yogi Berra, who each had nine career grand slams, for sixth place on the Yankees all-time list. He hit eighth that day, but at the age of 39, he became the second oldest player to ever hit a grand slam for the Yankees. Jose Cruz was 40 when he blasted a grand slam in 1988.

The highly competitive Posada was able to appreciate this day in a much different way than so many of his successful days in the past, and in a way, it relaxed him for the rest of the season.

"The fans were so supportive," Posada said. "I have to give them a lot of credit. They've been so supportive my whole career. I play for them, I really do."

"I'm grateful," he added. "I'm really happy that I got a chance today. I had the opportunity to help out today. I'm just taking it one day at a time. I'm hoping I'm playing again tomorrow. I really can't look ahead. I have to take each day as it comes and hope that I am in the lineup."

Posada's message was clear. He was basically imploring Girardi to put him in the lineup as DH, and by the time the playoffs had rolled around, Girardi did just that against right-handers.

Girardi had to find a way to get his aging players in games and still keep the Yankees moving forward as a team. That is just one of the challenges he faces as Yankees manager.

16.

ALL SYSTEMS JOE

KEVIN LONG IS a magical batting coach. Under his tutelage Curtis Granderson has become an explosive hitter, setting career highs in home runs (41), RBIs (119), and runs (136), leading the majors in runs and ranking second in home runs and fourth in extra-base hits (77) in 2011.

Long has tapped into Robinson Cano's potential and has helped make him an MVP candidate as the second baseman hit .302 with 104 runs, 46 doubles, 28 home runs, and 118 RBIs in 2011.

Alex Rodriguez, who suffered through an injury-plagued 2011, swears by Long. "It's amazing to watch Kevin work his magic," A-Rod explained. "There's no one like him. He can make in-game adjustments that are just amazing. I always say he's the best in the business."

Rodriguez thinks so much of Long that he wrote the introduction to Long's book, *Cage Rat*, thanking Long for all his hard work.

None of that magic just happens. Walk into Yankee Stadium five hours before a game, and Long is often on the field, doing the "home run" drill with a couple of his hitters. This is done in addition to the usually daily batting routine, which includes work with the tee, front toss, side toss, net drill, short bat, pitching machine, and many other drills that are the avenues to success that Long uses to get the most out of his hitters. The most interesting drill is the home run drill, simply because of the circumstances surrounding the drill.

This is not done in a batting cage behind the Yankees dugout, where the ball is just hit into a net. This drill is done on the field in an empty stadium; and when it is done right, balls are clanking all over the upper-deck seats.

What Long does is take a screen, one that is used to protect fielders during batting practice, and if the batter is left-handed, Long sets the screen just on the edge of the outside portion of the plate, along the black. He then walks in front of the plate, about one-third of the way to the pitcher's mound, stands behind another screen and zips balls to the hitters over the inner-half of the plate, using an underhanded motion.

The purpose of the drill is to shorten the hitter's swing, keep the hitter's hands inside the ball, work on balance (staying back and staying centered), and to do all that the hitter can to use his core. A long swing and too much forward movement create a lot of missed opportunities; a short swing to the ball creates a lot of success. Long stresses that the hitter make strong use of his lower half in this drill. Cano loves the drill and can often be found on the field working with Long several times a week on it. The second baseman doesn't wait until he gets out of sync, he uses this drill to stay in sync, and his success over the last few years is a direct result of his extended work with Long, who became the Yankees hitting coach in 2007.

That home run drill pays off in many ways. The Yankees led the majors in home runs in 2011 with 222. The only other teams to crack the 200 home run mark were the Rangers (210) and Red Sox (203). The Yankees also were second in runs scored with 867, eight runs behind the Red Sox.

One other thing about Kevin Long: he may be the most positive person on the face of the Earth. He never uses the term "slump," and he is always enthused about his hitters, preaching the positive.

Long's home run drill is just one of the systems in place on a Joe Girardi–managed ballclub. Girardi allows his coaches to work, and there is a system to that work. Girardi does not micromanage. He allows his coaches to guide the ballplayers. He is sure of their ways and has faith in his coaches, just as he has faith in his color-coded binder with all the matchups, stats, and revealing numbers.

It's proven to be a winning combination.

"Joe's strengths are obviously his ability to lead and use the people who surround him to help him lead," Long explained of what is at the heart of the Yankees' teaching philosophy. "For instance, he will very rarely post a lineup without talking to me first, and to me, that is a strength of his, going to his coaches and trusting his coaches. He'll ultimately have the final say, but I don't think every manager out there does that."

A lot of managers just write out a lineup, have their bench coach copy it onto the lineup sheet, and then post it to a clubhouse door. However, Girardi likes to take in information and work off of it. It is not his way or the highway. In this age of Sabermetrics, there are a lot of teams where the front office essentially gives the manager the lineup; the manager is a middleman. That's not the case here. Girardi will work with the front office, but he will take information on his lineup from his coaches, as well.

With a background in engineering, Girardi is not about to just throw together a lineup. A lot of thought goes into what he does, and through the years he has unlocked some pretty interesting lineups. When he moved leadoff hitter Johnny Damon to the second spot in the lineup and put Derek Jeter first, that was a key to a lot of the Yankees' offensive success in 2009, the year they won their 27th world championship.

Damon was a leadoff hitter for most of 2008 for Girardi. At the end of September, Girardi dropped Damon into the two-hole and then ran with the experiment the following spring when he was trying to get Jorge Posada some extra at-bats in a spring training game. He put Posada first and Damon second. Girardi liked what he saw that day, and by the start of the 2009 season, Damon was batting second with Jeter leading off, and the Yankees' offense was much better as a result.

When Girardi made the move, he stated a number of times that "Johnny is really good at getting runners over."

Clearly, the move was made to keep Jeter from hitting into so many double plays, as well. The move made sense on several levels, and Damon also pointed out that the move allowed him to really go for the long ball every once in a while. The inner Damon loves to go deep.

"Hitting second allows me to drop the hammer a little bit more," Damon said at the time, with a sly smile. Every player loves to go yard.

The move also made sense because speedy Brett Gardner was batting ninth at the time, and with Damon batting first, that would make it easier on opposing managers to face two lefties in a row. Having Jeter's right-handed bat at leadoff took away that advantage, and Girardi did not want to give the opposing manager a strategic advantage late in the game. Jeter also came into that season with a higher on-base percentage than Damon, so he could handle the leadoff spot from that perspective, as well.

Long endorsed the idea from the start, saying, "Maybe we can manufacture some more runs. I'm all for it."

The move did just that, created more runs. In 2008 the Yankees finished 10th in runs with 789. The next season they led the major leagues in runs with 915. It was a smart move.

In spring training in March of 2009, Girardi said he was toying with the idea of having Jeter bat leadoff and Damon bat second. Don't believe it. Girardi does not "toy" with ideas. There is a lot thought behind every last move. Nothing just happens in the Yankees lineup.

"Joe gathers information and he sorts through it," Long explained. "He makes very educated decisions, and that is what you want your leader to do. You want him to do what's best for the ballclub."

That is Girardi's job. That is what he is supposed to do. That is how systems work best.

Girardi thinks the Yankees have the best coaching staff in baseball. The Yankees brought all the coaches back for the 2012 season. In addition to Long, there is first-base coach Mick Kelleher, nicknamed "Killer," one of the nicest people in baseball, who also serves as the infield instructor. Kelleher spent time with the Pirates and the Tigers as a coach.

Larry Rothschild, a former manager, is the pitching coach. The 2011 season was his first with the club, and he helped guide what looked to be a shaky pitching staff at the start of the year to one that posted the fourth-lowest ERA in the AL with a 3.73 mark and led the AL in strikeouts with 1,222. Rothschild spent the previous nine seasons as pitching coach with the Cubs and is in his 38th season in professional baseball as a player, coach, or manager.

Mike Harkey, a former pitcher, is Girardi's bullpen coach. He was Girardi's bullpen coach with the Marlins, as well, in 2006. Harkey spent six seasons coaching in the Padres organization from 2000 to 2005 and is the coach who is closest to Girardi. He is essentially a second pitching coach and works directly with the pitchers warming up to come into the game. He has to make sure they are ready, mentally and physically.

Tony Pena is Girardi's bench coach and, like Girardi, is an ex-catcher. He is entering his seventh season as a Yankees coach. He managed the Royals and in 2003 was named the Manager of the Year by the Baseball Writers Association of America. He led the Royals to an 83–79 record that year, the sixth-best turnaround in major league history following a 100-loss season. He was a five-time NL All-Star over his 18-year major league career and is second in line behind Girardi, not only as bench coach but as the coach in the best physical condition. He is a tremendous batting practice pitcher, as well.

Rob Thomson is the Yankees' third-base coach and oversees the Yankees outfielders, who combined for the sixth-best fielding percentage in 2011 with a .989 mark. Thomson is from Canada and managed three games for the Yankees in 2008. He became the first Canadian manager in the majors since George "Mooney" Gibson with the Pirates in 1934. Four hours before a game you can usually find Thomson on the computer. Thomson takes care of spray charts, schedules, lineup cards, and is essentially the organization coach.

This is a staff that has bonded well and knows what is expected of them and what is expected in New York. This is a coaching staff that has its eyes wide open, and Girardi appreciates each one as a coach and individual.

Perhaps one of the things that Girardi can work on in the future is to somehow get MLB to schedule more day games for the Yankees, as they were 44–12 (.786) in 2011 in day games, the highest winning percentage in day games since 1900, according to the Elias Sports Bureau.

The Yankees also tied the Rangers for the best home winning percentage in the AL with a 52–29 record (.642), but despite all that, it didn't work out in the Yankees' favor in the five-game series with the Tigers when the Yankees lost the last game at home in the ALDS.

No matter what kind of system you have in place and no matter what the numbers say, sometimes the game goes its own way. It's not a science project. It's baseball. And that is one of the reasons Girardi is always there to back up his players. He realizes that sometimes things don't go your way.

"I think he is really fair with the players," Long said, listing Girardi's strengths as a manager. "I think he is more than fair with his coaching staff and trusts his coaching staff. Deep down inside, he is a great person. He cares about individuals. He wants them to be probably better people than baseball players, and all the best leaders I've played behind or been associated with, that's what they do. He's got those characteristics.

"There's a human side that is not all about the numbers," Long revealed. "He's going to go through the numbers and look at them. But he takes into consideration, 'How beat up is a guy? When can we give him a day off?'"

All that makes Girardi a strong leader, but here is what separates him from some other leaders.

"At the end of the day," Long explained, "he is very content with whatever decision he makes. That is because he puts in a lot of time and effort into those decisions."

Girardi is content with the decision he makes. He does not second-guess himself or his coaches when things don't work out. That is admirable.

Girardi and Long do not look at a situation through the same prism. "He'll look at pitching matchups and all that. I don't do that," Long said. "I go more on how a guy's swing is. 'Okay, this guy is swinging the bat good right now, this guy is not.' And Joe will look at matchups."

It is the best of both words, the expertise of what his coaches see and know, and what the data reveals to Girardi.

"I'm not as analytical as he is," Long said. "I have a good feel for the player. Joe has a good feel for the other, and at the end of the day he'll go, 'What's your gut? What would you do?' And I'll give him my gut feeling, and it's not just me, he'll take input from everybody."

Long's opinions on his hitters and Rothschild's opinions on his pitchers weigh a little bit more because that is their area of expertise. It is not all data and gut feelings for the Yankees coaching staff.

Where there is down time, usually on the plane, a card game will get started, and Girardi will watch the inner workings of the game. "He enjoys that rather than being in the mix," Long said with a smile. "He'll make comments. He is enjoying it. He is enjoying the fact that we're having fun, and we're relaxed. That probably takes some of the pressure off. The last thing you want to do is get on the plane and grind on baseball some more. There has to be a part of you that is away from the game for a time.

"For Joe, that is what his family does for him," Long said. "That is a big strength of his. He is able to get away from the grind of everyday New York baseball and enjoy his family. I think that is so important. It gives him a release from the everyday grind. It should be No. 1. You only get one chance at family. Obviously being the Yankees manager is a big deal. It's something he enjoys and really loves doing."

Girardi did not hand-pick this coaching staff, but through the years, he has built a strong relationship with his staff. Girardi gets along well with all his coaches, but he is closest with Mike Harkey.

"We go back to the minor leagues when we were roommates," Girardi said of their days together in the Cubs organization. "We've been there the whole way through. His kids growing up and me laughing at him when he was a young father with his kids, and yelling at his kids; and now it's me, it's the other way around. His kids are almost grown; and now it's me, he's laughing at me. Our relationship has been tight from day one, and I really can't tell you why. It's just a pitcher-catcher thing that we got along great. And the funny thing is we are complete opposites. It's amazing, a lot of my close friends are opposites, like Dante Bichette."

Opposites attract in baseball.

"Relationships are built over time," Long said. "Joe pays attention to our fantasy football stuff. He is really into college football. He will give us predictions, like he said Florida State would beat Oklahoma. He was wrong. So I like to throw it in his face and go back and tell him, 'You couldn't have been more wrong on that.' And that's fun to tell him."

The expectations are always huge in New York. The Yankees have made the postseason in 16 of the last 17 years. In the regular season they have finished first 47 times in their long and glorious history, the most of any North American sports franchise.

"I think there are a lot of players who would go through a brick wall for him," Long said of Girardi. "They respect his decisions. They respect his decision-making process and how he goes about it. It's really in the best interests of the players. When your manager truly believes in you as a player, has your back, that makes it easier to play. He's been able to build that over time.

"Alex [Rodriguez] thinks the world of Joe, and that's because Joe has always taken care of Alex," Long said. "Joe makes sure he talks to the players. He'll ask, 'How do you feel about this? Not just about the player himself, but like, 'What do you feel about the lineup today?' When you communicate and talk to the players, they feel like they are a part of it, and that is what you want. You want everybody to feel like they are a part of it. Whether we do good or we fail, we're all in it together."

Jason Giambi played for Girardi in 2008. That was the slugger's seventh season as a Yankee after coming over from the A's as a free agent. The first six seasons were under Joe Torre, a future Hall of Fame manager, and then came the change to Girardi.

"Joe Girardi was great," Giambi, now with the Rockies, explained of that season when he hit 32 home runs and drove in 96 runs. The Yankees finished in third place in the AL East with an 89–73 record. The Rays won the division with a 97–65 record with the Red Sox grabbing the wild-card by going 95–67. The Yankees suffered some key injuries, and the starting rotation was short to begin with when the Yankees did not land Johan Santana that off-season. That was the last year of Yankee Stadium, as well. It was a time of transition as the Yankees missed the playoffs.

"I played against Joe," Giambi explained. "He was a bench coach for us. He was very knowledgeable of the game, could control the game. Had the respect of not only his peers but of the opposing players.

"We all knew as players that when Girardi was going to be behind the plate, it was going to be a tough day because he did his homework. He was going to really work the hitters. You had to really think along with Joe how you were going to hit that day. He would change it up."

It was a chess match with Girardi calling the pitches, Giambi said. It's not always that way. Some catchers put themselves first and call pitches they can handle with runners on base, pitches that could make it easier to throw out a runner, but that was never the way for Girardi. The pitcher came first.

When Girardi made the switch to coaching and managing, it was pretty seamless, Giambi noted. "He had a good rapport with the players," Giambi said. "That first year of managing, even though we didn't make the postseason, I personally think he did a great job. The hard part for him was that when he first got in there he was replacing a Yankees great in Joe Torre, and I think he wanted to be different. He didn't want to be the same as Joe, and I don't blame him. Then we had some injuries.

"The fact we didn't make the playoffs took all the pressure off, and he was able to just be himself," Giambi said.

There was a learning curve for Girardi, and he eventually made the most of it, Giambi said.

"I still kept in contact the next year when they won the World Series and all the guys were telling me, 'He's awesome. It's a totally 'different guy' than that first year when we had a lot of adversity. A-Rod went down, pitchers went down, we didn't really sign anybody with all the young kids—with Phil Hughes, Ian Kennedy, and Joba Chamberlain—guys were injured. It was a tough year for Joe because it was a transition year, but he was awesome. I really enjoyed having him as manager that first year. He talked a lot to you, that's the one thing he does so well, that communication level. He went out of his way to keep you informed, and he had a game plan. Like he'd say, 'I need you to play the next 10 games, but I'll give you a DH day. I need you at first because Hideki [Matsui] comes back, and I want to DH him for those days. I need to give A-Rod a rest, and then I'll DH you for a week. Can you make it through the next 10 games?'"

With Girardi, there is always a plan.

"He really had it all thought out, just great rapport, he kept it light," Giambi explained. "He played for Joe [Torre] and understood what Joe Torre always did for us. Joe Torre would say, 'Listen, there is enough pressure playing in this town, you don't need any pressure from me.'

"Girardi took that to heart, he realized that from playing under Joe."

Giambi pointed out that no matter how much you prepare, it is so much different going from "copilot" in New York to "pilot."

"Just think, you are in the hot seat, and it's your first year replacing a Yankees legend. I think Joe just wanted to be a little more different," Giambi said. "That first spring training, he kind of ran our asses off, and it kind of backfired on him a bit, we got some early injuries. But we all knew what he was doing. He wanted to be different, and why wouldn't you? You want to be your own guy, especially in that town. You don't want to be second fiddle. He learned from Joe that you want to take control, take the reins, and that's what it takes in that town.

"That's what George Steinbrenner did. He took the reins and said, 'I'll take the ups, I'll take the downs.' And I think that's the great thing about Joe Girardi, he is such a good human being, and he said I need to do this differently, I need to do that differently. That's the biggest thing I love about him. He went into that year and established himself, and we loved him for it. We rallied around him, we just had so many injuries, but we were right there at the end.

"If we could have just had an extra two weeks...but it was a great time."

Girardi's first Yankees team got off to a slow start, 28–27 after the first two months of the season, but they finished 61–46 the rest of the way, and by September were rolling at 17–9. Like Giambi said, just a few more weeks would have made a big difference, but the major league schedule waits for no team.

The Yankees carried that September success into 2009, and it all came together for the Yankees and Girardi that following season. They have not missed the postseason since that first season under Girardi. The Girardi system has paid off in many ways.

Long said that working for Girardi is a pleasure because he is not hovering over him all the time. "I feel very fortunate. I guess some managers will go down to the cages and watch the hitting coach work. He doesn't do that. He doesn't dabble into my field at all.

"He wants to learn. You ask him about a hitter's backside, he'll know. Before he met me, he wouldn't have paid attention."

Essentially, a hitter's backside has to turn into the swing to have success.

Noted Long, "Joe will watch a hitter now who isn't doing that and say, 'K-Long, no backside.' That means he's paying attention to what I teach. He'll ask me questions about what I am looking at in specific instances. He takes it in and processes it."

Girardi does not walk up to Long and try to tell him his hitting business. "He'll ask me, 'What do you see?'" Long said. "He trusts me."

And there is another bonus to that approach of letting the coaches work in their own way without getting in the way.

"He can reinforce what we are trying to do," Long said. "He can go up to a Nick Swisher and say, 'Your stride is really short. I really like how your leg kick is under control.' In that way he can say some things that we are trying to work on in the cages, and that helps. There is a lot of time and effort put into it."

By the end of a season, a coaching staff is exhausted from the long year that begins in mid-February. After a few weeks rest, though, Long is right back at it, and Girardi allows him to visit with the players in the off-season to work on specific improvements.

Long knows how difficult a job Girardi has and sometimes sees the mental and physical wear and tear on him. "That job cannot be easy," Long said, noting the intense media scrutiny in New York. At the end of the season, Girardi wants to make sure that his team is as healthy as possible. With an aging team like the Yankees, that is a must. "There are days that he gets frustrated, and he'll say something like, 'I can't believe that they are on me about trying to get my players healthy,'" Long explained.

Criticism was tossed Girardi's way at the end of the 2010 season because the Yankees seemed content to get to the playoffs as the wild-card instead of going all out to win the division. The Yankees got in as a wild-card that year and made it to the ALCS. In 2011 the Yankees won the AL East, but never got out of the first round.

Being healthy is paramount to Girardi.

"His position is always scrutinized," Long said. "But he always has the best interests of the players and the organization as his top priority. That's why I like working for him. That's why I like coming into the clubhouse and spending time with him. He creates a very family-like approach. And when he has Family Day, that says it all right there; he wants to have your family around. You have to have people you can trust, and there is no one you can trust more than your family. When you need somebody to bounce things off of or share your frustrations with, it is good to have your family around. Joe never points fingers. He's got a really good grasp of our team, and that comes over time."

It is good to have a family atmosphere in the clubhouse, Long said.

"We have the highest payroll, so everybody expects us to win," Long explained. "Boston is going through a little bit of that right now. Just because you have all this stuff doesn't mean you are going to win. You are giving yourself the best shot, but over the long haul, you have to try to get the players better, too. At the end of the day, all that matters is winning the championship."

When the Yankees won the world championship under Girardi in 2009, one of the first players to seek out the manager was Rodriguez. A-Rod announced of that team, "Twenty-five guys bought into Joe's system and did a phenomenal job."

For Girardi, it's always about everyone doing their job. He wants the Yankees to be able to rely on one another in good times and when the team struggles. It starts long before the game starts. It starts in the clubhouse and training room where he checks in on the players daily. He wants to make sure that his players have the right mental approach and are physically healthy and even went so far as to ban certain sweets from the clubhouse.

The AL East is home to some tremendous managers, and the challenges will only get more difficult for Girardi.

Tampa Bay's Joe Maddon is the only one who has been at the job longer in the AL East than Girardi. Maddon started in 2006. In 2011 he won the AL Manager of the Year award for the second time in the last four years, guiding the low-payroll Rays' to their historic comeback and the wild-card win over the Red Sox. Girardi came to the Yankees two years later. Buck Showalter took over the Orioles for the last 57 games of the 2010 season. John Farrell, who was Terry Francona's pitching coach in Boston, began with the Blue Jays in 2011. Bobby Valentine is now in command of the Red Sox, getting the job in December 2011, just before the winter meetings.

Each manager in the AL East has his own style. There will be some of the best baseball minds in the AL East dugouts, matching wits with one another. It will continue to be a fascinating division. Valentine is much more talkative than Girardi and is not afraid to take an issue to the media.

Valentine will clearly be on the attack, something that Red Sox president Larry Lucchino prefers. Valentine will try to wake up the Red Sox, who have really lost their way. The Red Sox have not won a playoff game since October 18, 2008, and missed the postseason the last two years despite their huge payroll.

This new kid on the AL East block, the 61-year-old Valentine, will make this rivalry something special. On the day he was hired, Valentine broke down his philosophy and how he expects to deal with players, with this piece of managerial wisdom: "The most unfair thing you can do is treat people who are different the same way," Bobby V. explained.

Valentine immediately began the process of rebuilding bridges with the players. By the end of the 2011 season, the Red Sox were a team going in different directions. In so many ways, ace Josh Beckett is the key to the Red Sox, not just the rotation, but setting a new clubhouse vibe.

Valentine had angered Beckett because of his comments about Beckett's slow pace of pitching on an ESPN broadcast against the Yankees in August when Valentine was a broadcaster.

Long, in an in-game interview from the dugout, had made comments saying how the extremely slow pace of Beckett threw off the hitters' timing, and Valentine ran hard with those comments during the broadcast, saying that Beckett should pick up the pitching pace and that the Yankees–Red Sox games were just too long. Valentine was correct in his criticism at the time. Beckett was pitching at a snail's pace and was doing it simply to make the hitters uncomfortable. In the future, baseball could fine pitchers for pace-of-game infractions, according to the new collective bargaining agreement. None of that made Beckett very happy.

In mid-December, Valentine said he had smoothed things over with Beckett and that the right-hander was more upset with Long's comments, thus setting up one more avenue of interest the Yankees and Red Sox will travel along in 2012. Kevin Long will be at the center of attention when the two teams meet. The Yankees–Red Sox rivalry is one that continues to grow in so many different ways.

You can be sure the Yankees will hear Valentine's voice next season on the field of play. "My voice carries," Valentine said. "I am emotional, I'm passionate, but I also am very committed, and I think that is something these guys are going to enjoy.

"When I wake up every day, I work out, when I work out, I make a plan. I'm going to do something good and exciting today," Valentine said of his life philosophy.

In many ways, that is Girardi's philosophy, too: do something good every day, make a difference, offer hope.

With these two passionate men in charge of two of the biggest rivals, this will be one wild ride in the AL East.

"We used to play the Yankees six games," Valentine said of his days with the Mets and that bitter New York rivalry. "I can't imagine 18 games [against the Yankees]. Is it like playing 50 games? I think it is. Those long games are about quality hitters. The Yankees are quality top to bottom, and the Red Sox are quality top to bottom, and that's why you get those wars.

"I haven't managed a game on the losing side for a long time, and I can tell you I am going to hate it when we lose," Valentine said. "I'm going to love all those firsts when a guy gets his first hit, his first win, all that kind of stuff. I'm still going to get frustrated when things aren't done in an excellent way, and I'm still going to try to get out early to try to correct every problem in the world and go to bed a little ticked off that I didn't do enough."

That is the life of a manager in the AL East, a place where even if you win the division and the most games in the American League, it is a failure if you don't go on and at least make it to the World Series.

That is Joe Girardi's world, too.

"Bobby is probably going to be a little different type of manager than Terry was," Girardi said at the 2011 winter meetings, measuring his words for impact as he often does. "Because every manager is going to have a different philosophy than the last guy, but a lot of your moves as a manager are dependent upon what type of players you have. If you got a bunch of guys who hit the ball out of the ballpark and are slow to first base, you are not all of a sudden going to become a base-stealing team. Time will tell how he is going to manage that club, and it is our job to pay attention."

The Yankees and Girardi and his coaching staff are paying attention, you can be sure of that. The engineer in Girardi is gathering information, processing it, getting ready for each showdown with Valentine and the Red Sox and the rest of the AL East.

17.

OF FOOTBALL, MILESTONE MEN, AND THE BOSS

ONE OF THE GREAT parts of being manager of the New York Yankees is to have a front-row seat for all the milestones that come in pinstripes, everything from Derek Jeter's 3,000th hit, to Mariano Rivera's record-setting career save, to other perks like being able to take Dante to a day of Jets practice and teach Mark Sanchez how to slide.

"Football was my true passion," Girardi admitted. "There is something to me about the building up to one game once a week, and I loved the contact. And I'm seeing that in my son, he really loves football. It's kind of scary, a little bit. There was just something about football that I really had a true passion for, but I knew I wasn't big enough or fast enough to play. I was recruited to some small schools to play, and I just said, 'No, I'm going to play baseball.' Our game is different. I loved football. But I was too small, and I knew I didn't have much of a future in the game."

Girardi certainly made the right choice, but that doesn't mean he would not want to do something special with football. If he could, this is what he would love to do one cool fall day at Ryan Field in Evanston, Illinois:

"I think I would like to go back to my alma mater, Northwestern," Girardi said with a smile. "I watched the job that Pat Fitzgerald does there, and I think he's tremendous, and the energy that he shows and how much his players adore him. I would like to be him for a day. No. 1, I'd have to get real good offensive and defensive coordinators."

Just stand along the sidelines and take it all in and be there to inspire his team—that would be a dream come true for Joe Girardi. Fitzgerald is all about energy and passion. Whether it is jumping into linebacker drills or teaching the freshman the proper way to sing the Northwestern fight song at the start of each academic year, Fitzgerald is a Wildcat all the way, much like Girardi, and there is so much to admire. Fitzgerald's Northwestern teams have been bowl-eligible for a program-record five straight seasons.

In so many ways, it comes back to passion with Girardi and just a pure love of sports and the character sports can bring out in someone. That's why Tony Dungy is one of Girardi's heroes. Late in the 2010 season, Dungy spoke to the Yankees. In recapping Dungy's message to the team that day, Girardi told Don Amore of the *Hartford Courant*: "Team, family. The things you go through as an athlete, basically, especially at this time of year."

"I admire him for his faith, his beliefs, the type of man he is," said Girardi, noting that he subscribes to Dungy's website. Girardi, like most coaches, enjoys bringing in athletes, coaches, and leaders to talk to his club and also arranged to have sprinter Michael Johnson speak to the Yankees.

Jets coach Rex Ryan is a Girardi fan. It doesn't hurt that Girardi grew up a huge fan of "Da Bears" and Rex's dad, Buddy, and the famed 46 Defense designed by Buddy Ryan. Rex also has an appreciation for Girardi because they both work in the same pressure-filled market, so he knows what Girardi is up against and how difficult life can be facing the New York media day in and day out.

In some ways, Girardi has brought a football coach's mentality to the Yankees. What happens in this clubhouse, stays in this clubhouse. Injuries are guarded like state secrets. Future decisions are rarely discussed in the media. They are talked about only after they happen.

The bombastic Ryan, of course, is not your typical football coach. He loves the spotlight of the media and makes it work for him because he believes it takes pressure off the players if most of the attention is on the coach and the coach is in the firing line. And, win or lose, he is not going to change his style. What you see is what you get with Ryan; he's no NFL cookie-cutter coach.

In one way, Girardi takes a similar approach. He would rather take the heat than have his players take the heat. That is a central part of his coaching philosophy.

Ryan is not afraid to do something different. He doesn't go by the same playbook as most other NFL coaches, and he got to the AFC Championship Game in his first two years with the Jets. So when Rex needed help with a specific issue, he reached out to the Yankees. His problem was that his young quarterback, Mark Sanchez, did not know how to slide to avoid being hit. Sanchez' movements were awkward, and he was putting himself in jeopardy every time he ran with the football. Sanchez is nicknamed "the Sanchise" and has much to learn, so he needs to stay healthy to get where Rex wants him to go as a quarterback. His health is as vital to the Jets as CC Sabathia's left arm is to the Yankees.

So one day Rex put a call in to the Yankees. This was early December 2009, and the Yankees and Girardi had just beaten the Phillies a month earlier for their 27th world championship.

If you want to learn how to slide, you talk to a baseball player, especially a catcher, who is not prone to slide head first, and Girardi jumped at the chance to go to a Jets practice to teach Sanchez how to slide, and to bring Dante along for the ride.

Ryan was impressed, saying of that encounter, months later, "Girardi is amazing." He never expected the manager of the New York Yankees to show up to help him. "When we were having the issues with Mark, I'm like, 'Let's just call the Yankees.' I had no idea that Joe Girardi was going to show up, but he did and he was awesome. He talked to our team and he was fantastic."

Girardi, making it a family affair, used Dante, who was seven at the time, to demonstrate the different sliding techniques as he ran through about 15 slides with Sanchez. Girardi wanted to teach Sanchez to be aggressive in the slide to lessen the chance for injury.

"Joe was very fast when he was a kid," said his youth league coach Dave Rodgers.

Sanchez admitted to reporters that day that he had a lot to learn about sliding, noting, "I've never been a slider. In baseball I slid head first. In football I've done the same thing or tried to get out of bounds or throw the ball away."

In the NFL a quarterback must learn to slide effectively, or else he will not be a healthy quarterback for long. Girardi, who evaluates every aspect of the game from an engineering perspective, taught Sanchez to slide with his right leg, but this wasn't just about a sliding lesson. The Jets got to see the other side of Girardi, the leadership side, the manager who is all about trying to unite his team for the tough days ahead, and the fun side of Girardi.

This was Girardi showing his leadership abilities, as when he was a youngster playing baseball with the Sea Merchants or in high school or at Northwestern, when he was essentially a player/coach for his college team. It never changes. You are either a leader or you are not.

Reflecting on that day, Ryan saw a much different side of Girardi than the public sees along the rail in the dugout. "This guy is funny, he's entertaining, he's passionate," Ryan said. "He's got everything. I think in baseball you have so many games, so you almost have to be a little different."

Ryan is right about that. Baseball is a marathon. And it really is about not getting too high or too low. It's about maintaining an even keel through the 162-game season and then what could be another month of playoff baseball in October.

In baseball, there is always tomorrow. Girardi knows that and plays that game better than most. Ryan recognized all this immediately. "No. 1, he's sharp as a tack," Ryan added. "Northwestern-educated. He's just so smart." But here is the key part, according to the Jets coach.

"Girardi is a real man's man, too," Ryan said. "You have to love this guy. How do you not? You look at him, and he is a leader. Not everybody can coach all those great stars—A-Rod, Jeter, Teixeira, Cano—and get them to perform every day and play as a team. He handles his players. And look how competitive the Yankees are as a team. He knows they are under a microscope every day, yet they go out and they compete every single day. That's the beauty of it, and it's a great reflection on him."

Ryan then paid Girardi this compliment, coach to coach. "If he wasn't a great manager in baseball, he would have been a great football coach," Rex said.

Maybe some Sunday Ryan will let Girardi prowl his sideline. Coaching is more than Xs and Os. It's more than matchups. It's more than color-coded charts that are posted every game on the Yankees dugout wall. It is handling players and igniting the competitive fire in any way you can as a coach or manager.

Ryan is a master at that end of the game. That is why so many NFL players want to play for Rex. He has his players' backs. Maybe sometimes, too much, and they take advantage of him. Girardi knows that it's all about having the players perform to the best of their capabilities, and he will usually give a player many opportunities to succeed or fail.

"This game is a hard game," Girardi said about baseball.

At the end of the day in both baseball and football, the only number that matters is the number of wins. Jets linebacker Bart Scott, who followed Ryan from Baltimore to the Jets and knows the coach better than any other player, offered this about Ryan's philosophy. "Our goal isn't to be the No. 1 defense in the league, it's to lead the league in wins," Scott explained.

Girardi has always said the ultimate goal is not to win the AL East, it's to win the World Series, and that is why he always emphasizes winning series. Win series during the season, and you will be in the playoffs, no matter what. Win those series in October, and you will be world champions. That is what he is all about. That is what the Yankees did in 2009.

The day that Girardi visited the Jets, he talked to them about unity and the ups and downs of a season. Said cornerback Darrelle Revis, "It was a great speech." Baseball and football have one central common theme, Scott noted: "Ultimately, it's about our belief in each other. We always believe we're in the football game until it says triple zeroes." Stay together as a team until the end. That is the same message that Girardi delivers to the Yankees. The Jets could not stay together as a team in 2011, and it cost them dearly.

Yankee Stadium sees more than its share of great coaches coming to visit. It is a magnet for coaches. One day in 2011, Kentucky basketball coach John Calipari came to visit. His son Brad, 14, is a huge Yankees fan. Calipari knows all about expectations. "I love Joe Girardi's temperament. When you're coaching, guys who have been under the gun and attacked a little bit become as hard as steel and just survive it, and he has. I just love his temperament. The first time I met him, he was terrific with me, and it was exactly how I envisioned it before I met him. I was asking him more questions than he was asking me. I learned a lot just from watching how he interacts with his players, especially how you respond when your team gets smacked down a little bit. That's what coaching is all about. He does a great job."

Each season is different. Each season brings its own set of problems and own rewards. In many ways the Yankees' 2011 season will be remembered for what Derek Jeter accomplished on July 9. In the third inning, he joined the 3,000-hit club with a home run on a 3–2 pitch from the Rays' David Price, an exclamation point to his incredible career. Jeter became only the 28th player to reach 3,000 hits, and amazingly, the first Yankee to hit that magic number. Jeter went 5-for-5 that day, including getting the game-winning single. It was amazing in every way.

"If I would have tried to write that script and given it to someone, I wouldn't have bought it, it's just one of those special days," Jeter said after the game. "Afterward, it was relief, I was excited, but I'm going to be honest with you, I was pretty relieved. I've been lying to you guys for a long time, saying I wasn't nervous and there was no pressure—there was a lot of pressure to do it here while we were at home."

Girardi noted, "This is already movie-ready. His 3000th hit is a homer, and 3,003 is a game-winner."

Jeter wanted to get his 3,000th hit at home at Yankee Stadium. He wanted his parents in the stands of Yankee Stadium, the place where he promised at the end of the disappointing 2008 season that the Yankees would make new memories in the new stadium.

On that night in 2008 as Jeter stood near the front of the mound surrounded by his teammates and his new manager, Joe Girardi, Jeter said to the last crowd, the 54,610 fans who came that memorable night: "For all of us up here, it's a huge honor to put this uniform on every day and come out here and play. And every member of this organization, past and present, has been calling this place home for 85 years. It's a lot of tradition, a lot of history, and a lot of memories. Now the great thing about memories is you are able to pass it along from generation to generation. And although things are going to change next year, we are going to move across the street, there are a few things with the New York Yankees that never change: that's pride, it's tradition, and most of all, we have the greatest fans in the world. We are relying on you to take the memories from this stadium, add 'em to the new memories that come at the new Yankee Stadium, and continue to pass them on from generation to generation. So, on behalf of the entire organization, we just want to take this moment to salute you, the greatest fans in the world."

With that, Jeter took off his cap. His teammates followed the captain's lead and did the same, saluting the fans. Jeter then put his left arm around Girardi's shoulder and walked toward the left field line, as the team followed him, to take in Yankee Stadium one last time as Frank Sinatra's "New York, New York" played triumphantly. The Cathedral was officially closed, but just as Jeter promised, new memories would move across the street.

There would be another world championship in the New Yankee Stadium in 2009. The New Yankee Stadium has taken on a life of its own, kind of an adult Disney World version of Yankee Stadium with over-the-top amenities. And for the players it has become a home run haven. On July 9, 2011, at 2:00 PM, with a home run against Tampa's Price, Jeter made a new memory that Yankees fans could pass along from generation to generation. It was an amazing moment, an amazing day in Yankees history, a true milestone.

Across the country in San Francisco, Mets manager Terry Collins was thrilled by Jeter's day. "If you wrote a story; that would be the ending to it," Collins said. "It was great not only for Derek Jeter, but great for baseball to have one of the true great players do what he did today and celebrate 3,000 hits. Incredible."

Collins then took the legend of Jeter one step further. "When he's going to retire," Collins explained, "his last game, he's going to get four hits, he's going to get the game-winner, he's going to make a play in the hole and make the jump-throw to first, nip the guy in the ninth inning, and the Yankees are going to win the World Series. The guy has had a magical career, and I'm not surprised he had a day like today."

No one was surprised. That is Derek Jeter, he makes baseball miracles happen.

Two series before the momentous event, Girardi said he wanted Jeter to make sure he took the time to take it all in, noting of his former teammate, "He's trying to put it out of his mind, and that is what he does with major accomplishments. But I hope he really enjoys it because of what he's done and what he's meant to this organization. Three thousand hits, you don't see it every day."

Then Girardi made this prophetic comment. "I hope that when he gets around 2,998 that he gets those two hits that day, so he doesn't have to talk about it, so we don't all have to talk about it. I hope it happens suddenly. Sometimes when you see those milestones like that, it can take a few days. Players don't necessarily want to talk about it. We know that Derek doesn't want to talk about himself. We've known that since 1996. So hopefully, it happens really quickly."

It happened quickly, and it happened in record style, with Jeter going 5-for-5, and the home run came against one of the best pitchers in the American League in the lefty Price. *Sports Illustrated* labeled the hit, "The Moment," putting those words on its cover with a picture taken from high up in the stands and capturing the swing and ball as it began its climb to the left-field seats. The Moment forever caught in time.

Of his closing-the-Cathedral speech, Jeter later admitted he was "scared to death" to take the microphone that night, but Jeter has always performed best under pressure in the biggest moments. That is his legacy.

Girardi said he was happy to be there to witness it. As a manager, though, Girardi knows he has a job to do and that is to get the most out of his players. That is why, when he was asked about milestones in general, he made this revealing comment: "The biggest thing about milestones is sometimes they get in the way a little bit. You have to get through it."

You get through it, you enjoy the challenge and the moment, you take it in, and then you move on to the next challenge. Girardi had a similar approach to Mariano Rivera's milestone save No. 602 on September 19 against the Twins, also at Yankee Stadium. That save broke Trevor Hoffman's career record of 601. Rivera enters the 2012 season with 603 saves. This is a record that may never be broken.

The closest active pitcher to Rivera is 276 saves behind him, Francisco Cordero. The only other active pitcher with at least 300 saves is Jason Isringhausen with 300. Next on the list is Frankie Rodriguez at 291. That's why he is the Great Rivera.

"It's remarkable at his age that he is still doing it so often for us and to be able to pitch so often for us," Girardi said of the 42-year-old Rivera, who accumulated 44 saves in 2011, a remarkable number that Girardi does not take for granted for one second. "That's a gift and a credit to the work that he puts in all the time, whether it's during the season, during the off-season. To think that we've seen two guys get 600 saves the last couple of years is even harder to believe."

As for No. 603 and what Rivera means to the Yankees, Girardi said, "It's a lot of wins for the Yankees, I know that. It's a lot of World Series championships, it's a lot of playoff bids. It's a number that I don't think we'll see broken in our lifetime. Will it happen one day? I don't know, but I'll be shocked if it happens in our lifetime. You have an inner peace when Mo comes into the game. That's the feeling."

The Twins stayed on the field that day and applauded Rivera. "I think it shows to baseball what Mariano has done, and I also think it shows the class of the Minnesota Twins. If I'm not mistaken, [Twins manager Ron Gardenhire] is the one who mentioned that Mo belonged in another league, years ago. Ron Gardenhire has always had his team first-class. I've never seen them not exhibit first-class behavior."

Girardi can look at Rivera from so many different perspectives. He was the teammate who saved the Yankees in all the big games. He was the closer who brought Girardi his first world championship as a manager. That season Rivera also saved 44 games in the regular season and another five in the postseason, including two saves against the Phillies. He didn't get the save in the final game because the Yankees won 7–3, but Rivera did get the final five outs. Girardi was not going to take any chances and blow that closing victory. He put the game and the ball in Mo's hands.

"You just feel he is going to get it done. I think about 2009 at 39 years old, [1⅔ innings) against the Phillies," Girardi said. "I don't know if we would have had him the next day, he had a bad rib and still did it, and I think that's why Mo is put in a different class."

Like Jeter, Rivera is in the Milestone Class, the best of the best. Beyond the 603 regular season saves, Rivera owns 42 postseason saves, including 11 World Series saves.

The biggest perk of all, of course, of being Yankees manager, is the championships. When Girardi and the Yankees won world championship No. 27 in 2009, he wanted his players to enjoy the accomplishment in so many different ways. This was much more than a parade through the Canyon of Heroes and those wonderful memories. When the championship rings were delivered the following season in the home opener, he was asked by WFAN's Sweeny Murti what he wanted his new players to take out of that precious ceremony.

"My guess is what they will take out of it is, 'I want one,' and that's a good thing," Girardi explained. "You look at the six new guys that we have, I don't think any of them have a championship ring. It will be something that they are going to want."

That is always the goal. Always take on the next challenge. That was what George Steinbrenner always wanted. If you won one year, the goal was to win the following year, and the work would begin before the parade was complete.

Three months after the Yankees got their last world championship rings, Steinbrenner died at the age of 80 on July 13, 2010. Girardi was in Anaheim to manage the All-Star team, and there were tears in his eyes that day as he explained what the Boss meant to him. "It's sad, it changes the day," Girardi said. He then mentioned not championships but how Steinbrenner cared about people. "This is a man who I don't think ever got enough credit for the way he cared about people. The way he gave people second chances and third chances. He really tried to make peoples' lives better. I know he changed my life completely.

"His toughness came out to me in expectations," Girardi explained. "I think the expectations that he had carried over into the clubhouse, and we had the same expectations as he did, which I think is the sign of his influence on all of us. But through that, I mean, he would needle me about Northwestern football, about who they were playing. He would needle me all the time, and had a way of making some light moments during some tough times or around playoff times. I enjoyed it. I never really felt that his expectations were overbearing. I felt he just wanted what all of us wanted—to win—and he was a pleasure to play for, and he's been a pleasure to work for."

Girardi is thankful that he was able to help Steinbrenner get his last World Series championship ring, the seventh of the Boss' career in 37 years of owning the Yankees. "I think winning the World Series meant a lot to him, but the next day he was back at work. He was like, 'Okay, how are we going to win next year?'" Girardi explained. "I really believe that he enjoyed it, but he stayed the course all the time. We experienced that in 1996. We won in 1996, and we were told that he was already planning for 1997 when they were planning the parade. How are we going to win this year? I think he truly loved it and probably felt that it was a huge accomplishment, but he never rested on it."

It was Jeter who presented the Boss with his final championship ring before the home opener on April 13, 2010, a 7–5 win over the Angels. Jeter and Girardi went to his private suite to present the Boss his ring. "It was fun," Jeter said that day. "None of us would be here if it wasn't for him. The stadium wouldn't be here if it wasn't for him. To present him with the ring, you know how much winning means to him, that's the only thing he cares about."

At the All-Star Game, Jeter mentioned that was the last time he saw the Boss and that he was planning to see him the day after the All-Star Game in Tampa. Looking back on that day, Jeter smiled and said, "I got the chance to tease him because he had an Ohio State ring, and I told him to take it off now and replace it with the Yankees ring. That's what you remember, those intimate moments. We had a lot of one-on-one moments."

"I've known him since I was 18 years old," Jeter added. "There's a respect factor because he's the owner, and I work for him, but we were more friends than anything. I'd go visit him in the off-season because we both live in Tampa. We would have bets on Ohio State–Michigan football games. I've been in trouble a couple of times. We've filmed commercials with him dancing. It's tough because he's more than just an owner to me. He's a friend of mine."

Girardi recalled the first time he met the Boss in 1996 after he came over from the Rockies, and he told this story with a smile: "It was really, really early in spring training, and Mr. Steinbrenner always had the perception of being an extremely tough man with huge expectations, and we were actually walking our little white Bichon on the grass, the beautifully manicured grass in spring training, and I thought, 'Oh, boy, he's going to let my wife and I have it.' He sat and talked to us and asked about the dog, and it was a totally different expectation than what I had. I think that was the first time I saw that he wasn't everything he was painted to be; there was a gentle side to this man. But I have to tell you—one of his athletes walking a little white dog—I was expecting something totally different."

George Steinbrenner's bark was always worse than his bite. "He's meant so much not only to this organization," Girardi said, "but to all of baseball."

18.

COUNTING ON CC AND CONTINUITY

THIS IS A NEW era for the Yankees. They still have the biggest payroll, but they are trying to make their money last and no longer are just spending money to make an impression or as a reaction to another team's bold move. If a player does not fit their needs, they will not go out and break the bank just because someone else made a monster purchase. This is not exactly fiscal restraint as much as it is fiscal responsibility.

Essentially, the Yankees are counting on CC Sabathia to carry the pitching staff. The big man will have to carry the big load. The Yankees will still buy the big-ticket item, but they will not be duped into spending money just to make it look like they are improving the team. That's when mistakes are made that can set the team back for years to come.

That means giving CC his money but waiting on the younger pitching talent to develop until another sure thing like Sabathia comes along on the free-agent market, as when the Yankees originally signed Sabathia on December 18, 2008. The Yankees are trying to develop two essential items as an organization, and that has been difficult for some fans to grasp. They must develop their young talent, like the Core Four that came along in the '90s, and develop patience as an organization. That is the message they are trying to get to the fan base. That is what Brian Cashman and the Yankees are trying to do these days, and it's not going to be easy because other teams have begun to spend like the Yankees used to spend. Newfound TV money has brought about the financial change. The Phillies' payroll is through the roof. After the 2011 season, the Angels went on a wild spending spree, signing slugger Albert Pujols away from the St. Louis Cardinals, the only organization that Pujols has ever known, and signing free-agent pitcher C.J. Wilson away from their division rivals, the Texas Rangers, who have become the new AL powerhouse, making it to the World Series in back-to-back seasons. The Tigers signed free agent Prince Fielder to a nine-year $214 million contract.

The Los Angeles Angels of Anaheim shelled out $254 million for Pujols, signing the free agent to a 10-year deal and another $77.5 million for the left-hander Wilson, a tidy one-night $331.5 million shopping spree by owner Arte Moreno—the kind of shopping spree that George Steinbrenner used to make for the Yankees. The Rangers responded by going after Japanese pitching sensation Yu Darvish, who could be phenomenal. Nolan Ryan's club wanted Darvish so badly they dropped $51.7 million into the laps of the Nippon Ham Fighters just for the rights to negotiate with the right-hander. They signed Darvish to a contract worth $60 million over six years.

All this means there will be even more pressure on Sabathia, who agreed to a five-year extension with the Yankees after the 2011 season that will pay him $122 million.

"CC is really appreciated here, not only by us, but by the fans," Joe Girardi said. "CC could spend a week on a team, and you'd fall in love with his personality, that's the type of guy he is. His value to the team is so important, the type of person he is. He seems to bring a group together. He hangs out with everyone. He's not a guy who is with a couple of guys. People want to be around him. I think that is important because during the course of the season everyone goes through tough times. But this is a guy you can count on, who you know is going to be the same every day and will be there for you, and that's extremely important."

That is the key for the Yankees. Sabathia is the kind of foundation pitcher that makes everything else possible. He loves playing for the Yankees and living in Alpine, New Jersey, with his wife, Amber, and their four children. It's about Competition and Contentment for Sabathia. That's the CC that matters most to him. In so many ways, he is a throwback, and that is why the Yankees wasted so little time in extending Sabathia's contract after the 2011 season, paying him $122 million over the next five years.

Having Sabathia anchor the pitching staff and the clubhouse is just what Girardi wanted to have happen. "It's absolutely great," Girardi said. "He's a better person than he is a player. He's great to have in the clubhouse. He's such a great teammate. You know exactly what you are getting. You are getting 20 wins a year out of this guy and 240 innings. Not too many people can do that in this world. He brings people together."

During his first three years with the Yankees and Girardi, Sabathia is 59–23 with a 3.18 ERA. He has pitched 705 innings during the regular season. In the postseason he has added another 61 innings with a 3.54 ERA. In the series against the Tigers in 2011, Sabathia did not get a win in two starts and a relief appearance as his ERA ballooned to 6.23. He is driven to do much better in the future for Girardi and the Yankees.

CC is the baseball glue for Girardi. The two have grown close, and Sabathia loves playing for Girardi, not only because of Girardi's knowledge about the game and his preparation, but also because of the way Girardi allows families to interact within the team. It is not just the player that is a Yankee; the entire family is wearing pinstripes. That is why Sabathia re-signed with the club, even though he could have opted out and gone to another team.

"That's one of the biggest things," Sabathia said. "With me hav-ing a big family, I'm pretty into my family and to have him be the way he is about his family and have a bunch of kids come in and running around and do whatever they want, it makes the guys feel comfortable. It makes us have a lot of fun all year long.

"I was always staying," Sabathia said. "It's a great situation, and Joe Girardi is a great manager to play for. His communication is great. He always wants to talk and make sure that everything is okay with you, with your family, with everything. Whenever you need time off, anything, he is there for you. That is a great feeling to have as a player because I have played for managers where that is secondary to them. But Joe puts family first. I think he feels that if we're good with our family, we can go out and perform to the best of our abilities."

That is the foundation of Girardi's philosophy.

Family is first for Carsten Charles Sabathia, and to see him with Amber and their two sons, Carsten Charles III (nicknamed "Little C") and Carter Charles, and two daughters, Jaden Arie and Cyia Cathleen, is to see a man who knows he is blessed. Many of his charitable efforts go toward helping children. His mother, Margie Sabathia-Lanier, also takes great pride in helping with his foundation, which is called PitCCh In. The foundation does much work in the New York area and in Vallejo, California, his hometown. Whether it is rebuilding baseball fields, helping to rebuild a women's community center, or helping senior citizens plant a new garden, CC, Amber, and Margie are pitching in on so many different projects and giving their time as much as their money. For Sabathia, it all comes back to family and being a father.

"It's so important to be a good parent," CC said. "My parents split when I was 12, but up until that time, my dad was there with me every day, playing catch, playing football, doing everything a dad was supposed to, a great role model. I had a tough time when they split, but my mom never badmouthed him, and that enabled us to get our relationship back, and I miss him to this day."

CC's father, Corky, passed away at the age of 47. Corky had his own demons to deal with and had a struggle with drugs, but in the end, father and son reconciled. Before Corky left the family, CC would often go to Raiders games and tailgate with his dad. In those years, the Raiders played in Los Angeles, so CC and his father would pack up the car at midnight and drive to L.A., arriving around 6:00 AM. "We'd tailgate, watch the game, and then head home," CC said of those precious times.

After they reconciled, when CC was in the Cleveland Indians organization, the two would tailgate at Raiders games in Oakland. Spending time with family is a gift.

Sabathia's mother worked the overnight shift at Travis Air Force Base near Vallejo so she could go to all of his events and make sure he stayed on the right path growing up. Her mother, Ethel Rufus, was also there to help raise CC. Margie, 52, is a tremendous athlete, as well, and would put on full catcher's equipment and catch CC's bullpen session up until the time he became a teenager and his fastball just became too difficult to handle. Mother and son also would have some great Ping-Pong battles growing up. "She's a fantastic athlete," CC said.

Abe Hobbs, CC's baseball coach at Vallejo Senior High, said CC's mother was always there to keep tabs on him. "I was coaching third one day, and he smashed his helmet to the ground," Hobbs recalled. "Before I could get across the diamond, his mother had already gotten to him to let him know that he should not be acting that way. She is a wonderful person and raised CC right."

His wife, Amber, noted, "CC has many jobs. He's a baseball player, he is a son, a husband, and a father. He will tell you that what's most important is being a father. I always tell him that baseball will be over seven, eight years from now; you are going to be a father for a very, very long time."

Girardi's wife, Kim, would say the same thing about Joe. The fact that Girardi has made the Yankees clubhouse so family friendly is an aspect of the Yankees that CC and so many other Yankees enjoy.

In his three years with the Yankees, Sabathia has won a World Series and has made it to the postseason all three years. *Continuity* is the new catchword for the Yankees, and Sabathia is completely on-board with that concept, saying, "I think that is a big reason why we've won. We continue to have a good clubhouse, and we continue to win because of his attitude."

The Yankees won 97 games in 2011, the most in the American League, with Sabathia leading the way, going 19–8 with a 3.00 ERA, and came up one win short in the ALDS against the Tigers. Sabathia will be 31 in 2012. He has pitched in five straight post-seasons. He is in the prime of his career and worked hard in the off-season to get into better shape because he does not want to go through the kind of postseason where the Yankees are eliminated in the first round as they were in 2011. "I came here to win championships," Sabathia said. He's won one championship. He wants more. He said he wants another parade.

The first four years of managing the Yankees may have been the most difficult for Girardi in one respect, as Yankees broadcaster Michael Kay pointed out. "I don't think it has been easy for Joe to manage guys he played with," Kay explained. "And I don't think it's been easy for him to manage guys who played for Joe Torre because they are two different guys. Eventually, that's going to be easier for him. I don't think the players on this team actually realize how many bullets he takes for them."

Girardi does not throw players under the bus. That is not in his makeup. He is not that kind of manager. He looks at himself as being there to offer another line of protection and support to his players. He will say that a player is going through struggles, but he always gives the impression that he believes in that player and is certain the player will turn it around. He is the eternal optimist even in the most difficult of circumstances.

Girardi often spent time defending A.J. Burnett. The right-hander went through another poor season, struggling to finish 11–11 in 2011 with a bulging 5.15 ERA. Burnett and Sabathia signed as free agents after the 2008 season. While Sabathia is 59–23 during his time with the Yankees, Burnett is only 34–35 with a 4.79 ERA and has allowed 81 home runs over the 584 innings that he has pitched for Girardi. Over his 705 innings, Sabathia has allowed 55 home runs. Burnett's problems can be related to his windup because he has so much side-to-side movement instead of being more direct and downhill toward home plate.

Burnett was at his worst in August 2011, posting an 11.91 ERA, the kind of performance that gets you bounced from a rotation. In a start against the Twins on August 20 at Target Field, Burnett lasted only 1⅔ innings and gave up seven runs. Yet, when Girardi came to get him from that game, Burnett flipped the ball to the manager and appeared to curse on the way off the mound to the dugout. After the 9–4 loss, Burnett said he was upset with the home plate umpire, D.J. Reyburn, but it looked as if he were upset at his manager for pulling him from the game.

Noted Michael Kay of that day, "I was more offended the way A.J. gave him the ball on the mound because Joe never ripped A.J. All he did was support the guy when everybody was against him. This guy should never be disrespected by his players because he never disrespects them."

Girardi makes a point to always respect his players. Girardi goes out of his way to keep all squabbles in-house. He's not Billy Martin in that respect. That's not who he is, and he is not going to apologize for taking the high road and not embarrassing his players publicly. Players respect that approach, and several times during the season Burnett acknowledged that Girardi had his back, which he deeply appreciated.

In the typical postgame interview, when Girardi takes his seat on the podium at Yankee Stadium or is sitting at the manager's desk in visiting clubhouses, he often points to mechanics as being the essence of Burnett's problems. "A.J. has always been a guy whose mechanics can be a little complicated at times because he has that big turn," Girardi has said time and again.

When Burnett shows displeasure at being taken out of the game, Girardi—who has spent his baseball life going to the mound, trying to get a troubled pitcher back on track—often passes it off as no big deal, offering a general comment such as, "Pitchers never want to come out."

Cashman signed Burnett to the five-year, $82.5 million contract before the 2009 season. By winning the world championship that season, Cashman believes the signing was a good signing. As for Burnett's personality, he noted early in the 2011 season, "A.J. cares. The great thing about him is that he is a deeply talented person. He's a professional to the media after every start. He wants to do well. And he's put himself in a position to be more consistent, that's all you can ask. I think we'll see that he will be. We feel he will have a real solid year for us. Our team strength is our offense and our bullpen. Our Achilles is the rotation, so any areas of under-performance in the rotation are going to hurt."

Many of Burnett's starts were painful. He would be breezing along and then lose his command. Despite all of Burnett's issues during the season, in the postseason, Girardi managed to get a good start out of the right-hander as Burnett came up the winner in the 10–1 victory over the Tigers at Comerica Park in Game 4 of the ALDS. Burnett pitched 5⅔ innings, allowing only one run, a home run by Victor Martinez in a game the Yankees had to win. Burnett did his job in the postseason, and that was most likely made possible by the way Girardi handled him during the season. He never quit on Burnett. The Yankees lost Game 3 in Detroit, so Burnett's win was their only road win of the series.

These days, more than ever, a team must stay together because there always will be issues on every team, and in the age of Twitter and social media, every issue is magnified. Everyone has an opinion and a message board on which to post that opinion. Everybody is a columnist, and everything is analyzed and often over-analyzed. During spring training, a bullpen session becomes big news with the media looking for every morsel of news available. Yes, teams have to stay together.

Rays manager Joe Maddon is able to get the most out of the talent he is given each year. "For us to be successful," Maddon said, "we have to embrace organizational philosophy, we have to all buy in, we have to all be on the same sheet of music, whatever you want to call it. We have to be that group. We are not going to be successful any other way, so being together for us is really, really important."

Being together has never been more important for teams. Looking ahead to the future, Girardi likes the makeup of the Yankees, a team that will now have to take on a beast in the Angels; prove they can beat the Rangers and Tigers, the two teams that knocked them out of the postseason the last two years; still battle their chief rivals, the Red Sox, rebuilt now with Bobby Valentine as the manager; and keep Maddon and his pitching-loaded young Rays at bay. The challenge grows every year for the Yankees and for Girardi as he tries to build another championship team.

"I like this team because I like how they seem to be able to fight back when things get tough," Girardi said, knowing there will be many tough times ahead for his team. "We've been through a lot of things. Think about what we went through this past year and the struggles we had with the Red Sox, and we end up winning the division. I think they do understand me better, and I will continue to understand them better. It takes time. Relationships take time. To fully understand your players, it takes time. I know one thing, I have a much better idea after four years than when I first walked in the door."

Girardi has grown as a manager and a person. He made adjustments after his first season and will continue to make adjustments. There is more continuity with the Yankees, and that is the essence of the new philosophy surrounding the team. Cashman and Girardi are working to that end and have brought new, hungry, homegrown talent into the clubhouse in younger players like pitcher Ivan Nova, who was 16–4 with a 3.70 ERA his rookie season. Those were the most wins of any rookie pitcher in the majors. The last Yankees pitcher to do better over the first 20 decisions of his career was a lefty named Whitey Ford, who produced an 18–2 record over his first 20 major league decisions. Girardi's ability to coax pitchers along, something he did his entire career as a catcher, paid off with Nova and others on the staff.

The plan is for the Yankees to continue to move young pitchers through the system, and names like Michael Pineda, Jose Campos, and Manny Banuelos should become prominent names in the future of the ballclub. Girardi and Cashman both know that for the Yankees to continue to make the postseason, they must develop young power pitchers. Girardi also did a good job of helping to develop young reliever David Robertson, who is the next closer for the team whenever Mariano Rivera finally decides to end his magnificent run. Girardi believes in all his players. "I want everyone in that room to believe that they can play a significant role in the playoffs," he said, just before the 2011 postseason started. Most of all,

Girardi feels he has a better sense of how to put his players in positions that will make them successful.

"You understand situations where your players can be successful," Girardi said of the advantage of having continuity and his four years of experience with the club. "You understand the signs when they are physically tired and when they need a day off or when they don't need a day off. You understand those things, and that's the importance of being together."

There is the importance of not taking anything for granted. "Our team doesn't take it for granted, and that's a tribute to our coaching staff," Girardi said. "They don't let them take things for granted."

It is a team game all the way around for Girardi. It's all a bit like raising a family. "I think it's important that you keep the family together," he said.

The Yankees' formula for success now includes adding a veteran starter they can pick up at a relative bargain, and Freddy Garcia fits that role perfectly. For Garcia, it's about using your brains as well as your talent. For Girardi, it's about having players who know how to make adjustments.

"Freddy has been great for us," Girardi said of Garcia, who is 24–14 over the last two seasons with the White Sox and Yankees. Over that same span, Burnett is 21–26. Reliable starting pitching can be found in different places, if you know where to look, and Cashman discovered gold in Garcia. "I think Freddy is very clever," Girardi added. "I think he understands how to pitch to the scoreboard. I think he understands how to pitch when runners are in scoring position. I think he knows how to pitch when nobody is on. I think he reads swings well. Freddy is very, very clever."

Call all of that situational pitching. Today's athlete is more physically gifted than past generations of athletes, but for the most part, the situational awareness of players, in all sports, is not as strong as it once was, and to find a player with situational awareness is a big plus. Remember, Girardi had to work to make himself the best he could be and had to think the game through. He understands that being clever can be a huge advantage to a pitcher.

After so many years of studying pitchers, Girardi breaks down that aspect of the game with this comment: "There's such a fine line sometimes in getting an out and giving up a base hit, and that's the bottom line in pitching. It always comes down to location. Sometimes you catch too much of the plate. The key is to keep those struggles short."

That is the only way to survive. Because Girardi has been around the Yankees for so long, going back to his playing days, and because of his serious demeanor, sometimes it is overlooked that he is still such a young manager. Entering the 2012 season, at the age of 47, he is the fifth-youngest manager in the majors behind only Cleveland's Manny Acta, Seattle's Eric Wedge, and newcomers Mike Matheny in St. Louis and Robin Ventura with the White Sox.

When the Yankees won the World Series in 2009, Girardi became the youngest Yankees manager to win a World Series. Over the last 36 years, only the Twins' Tom Kelly in 1987 and 1991, the White Sox's Ozzie Guillen in 2005, and the Mets' Davey Johnson in 1986 were younger than Girardi was when the Yankees won in 2009. He continues to grow as a manager every day. One of the aspects he has improved upon is taking a longer view during the season, and that is not easy for someone who hates to lose. "I think you have to be careful that when you lose a couple days in a row or three in a row, you don't push a panic button," Girardi said during one such losing streak in 2011. "This is a good team. Every guy is going to go through struggles, you just hope they don't do it together."

The Yankees did not have a flashy off-season following the 2010 season. Did Girardi wonder if the Yankees would have enough to win 97 games and the AL East heading into 2011 season? "We weren't sure what our rotation was going to be," he said, looking back in the last week of the season. "We knew we had CC coming back, and we knew we had Phil Hughes coming back, an 18-game winner, and that we had A.J. and Nova, who we felt, was going to make big strides, but we weren't quite sure after that. We felt our bullpen was going to be very strong even though we never saw [Pedro] Feliciano, but there were a lot of question marks."

Hughes went backward, winning only five games and producing a 5.79 ERA. The No. 2 and 3 starters, Hughes and Burnett, were a combined 16–16, yet the Yankees won 97 games. "I'm not surprised that our guys got it done," Girardi said. "This is a group that knows how to win. This is a group that is resilient and is not going to panic when things aren't going our way for a few days. They know how to get it done."

There is an art to that, and the 2012 Yankees will have to figure out a way to get it done in the regular season and then find postseason success, something these Yankees did not find. They will have to find a way to come up with the big hit when needed. Alex Rodriguez is going to have to stay healthy and supply the big postseason bat, something he did in 2009, not the A-Rod who hit .111 in the 2011 postseason and batted only .191 in the regular season after returning from knee surgery. He must do all that at the age of 36, and Girardi must be sure to rest Rodriguez and the other aging Yankees as much as possible during the season to keep them strong.

The road will not be easy for the Yankees or Girardi. Huge question marks remain, but Girardi feels that the continuity the Yankees have built over his first four years on the job will carry them to the postseason once again. Joe Girardi is ready for this baseball challenge more than ever. This is no ordinary Joe.

ACKNOWLEDGMENTS

GETTING ALL THE PIECES of this book to fit together became quite the puzzle. Let me start by thanking Chris Shaw and Dave Blezow, the men who run the greatest sports section in the world, the *New York Post*; fellow *Post* columnist Steve Serby for his advice early on in the project; and Tom Bast, Adam Motin, and Steve Mandell for getting the biggest pieces of this puzzle to fit.

Thanks to those I interviewed for being so gracious with their time and memories, starting with those who knew Joe Girardi from his days growing up in East Peoria through his college years at Northwestern University: Todd Mervosh, Dave Rodgers, Paul Stevens, and Ron Wellman.

So many people answered so many questions during this project, first and foremost, Joe Girardi. The long list includes Don Zimmer, Joe Torre, Don Baylor, Brian Cashman, John Filippelli, Michael Kay, John Sterling, Tino Martinez, Jason Giambi, Jason Zillo, Kevin Long, Tony Pena, Yogi Berra, Rex Ryan, John Calipari, Joe Maddon, Bobby Valentine, Larry Lucchino, David Cone, Dwight Gooden, Dave Eiland, the MLPBA's Michael Weiner and Greg Bouris, CC Sabathia, Alex Rodriguez, Mark Teixeira, Brett Gardner, Derek Jeter, Curtis Granderson, Mariano Rivera, Jorge Posada, Gene Michael, A.J. Burnett, Ed Lynch, Johnny Damon, Mark Grace, Margie Sabathia-Lanier, Amber Sabathia, Ray Negron, Aris Sakellaridis, Barrett Esposito, Joe Castellano, Serena

Girardi, Terry Collins, Dave Barnett, Tracy Ringolsby, and Gerry Fraley.

Thanks also to the Yankees, Hank Steinbrenner, Randy Levine, Lonn Trost, Brian Cashman; all the coaches—Kevin Long, Tony Pena, Mike Harkey, Mick Kelleher, Larry Rothschild, and Rob Thomson—who always take the time to explain the little details; assistant GM Billy Eppler; VP of amateur scouting Damon Oppenheimer; video coordinator Charlie Wonsowicz; the club's public relations department: Jason Zillo, who is the driving force behind Hope Week, Jason Latimer, Michael Margolis, Lauren Moran, Kenny Leandry, Alex Trochanowski, and Germania Dolores Hernandez; executive director of team security Edward Fastook, Mark Kafalas, and historian Tony Morante. Also, Joseph Avallone of the Creative Group, Jeff Idelson, and Brad Horn of the National Baseball Hall of Fame and Museum, Dave Buscema, Jack Curry, Jack O'Connell, and MLB's senior VP of public relations Pat Courtney.

SOURCES

Books
Long, Kevin, with Glen Waggoner. *Cage Rat*, HarperCollins, 2011

Newspapers
Chicago Sun-Times
Chicago Tribune
Denver Post
Hartford Courant
New York Times
Rocky Mountain News
USA Today

Magazines
Northwestern Perspective
Sports Illustrated
Team Publications
Yankees 2011 Media Guide
Yankees 2011 Postseason Media Guide
Yankees Magazine

Websites
Alzheimer's Association (www.Alz.org)
ASAP Sports (www.asapsports.com)
Baseball-Reference.com (www.baseball-reference.com)
The Daily Northwestern (www.dailynorthwestern.com)
ESPN (www.espn.com)
Goat Riders of the Apocalypse (www.chicagonow.com)
Harvard Business Review (www.hbr.org)
Major League Baseball (www.MLB.com)
NJ.com (www.nj.com)
YES Network (www.yesnetwork.com)

Wire Services
Associated Press
Elias Sports Bureau